After the Fishermen

How did Jesus train his disciples?

About the Author

Terry Young was born in New England to parents who were missionaries in the Middle East. In 1970, the family returned to the UK and settled in the Midlands, where Terry enjoyed a spot of schooling and a spell at the local Redbrick. He read physics and electronics, followed by a PhD in physics.

Moving into industrial research and development, Terry has worked with innovation at various levels, usually involving communication components, systems or applications. When he wrote this, he worshipped at a local church that was good at encouraging people and he was on the leadership team for just over a decade. He has now moved on and is an academic.

Terry and Danielle married in 1988 and have three sons.

Partnership

After the Fishermen

How did Jesus train his disciples?

Terry Young

Published for

by

PATERNOSTER PRESS

Copyright © Terry Young 2004

First published 2004 by Partnership and Paternoster Press

09 08 07 06 05 04 03   7 6 5 4 3 2 1

British Library Cataloguing in Publication Data
A catalogue record for this book is available from the British Library.

ISBN 0-900128-28-3

Cover design by Paulo Baigent.

Typeset by Profile PPS Ltd, Culmdale, Rewe, Exeter.

Produced by Jeremy Mudditt Publishing Services, Carlisle,
and published by Partnership and Paternoster Press,
PO Box 300, Carlisle, Cumbria CA3 0QS.

Printed and bound in Great Britain
by Bell and Bain Ltd, Glasgow.

To dearest Dani
who entertained the boys and got on with the things I should have
been doing while I was writing this

Contents

Preface

Getting Started

I was perched on one of those high barstools somewhere between nine and half-past bed time. It had been the first day of a management training course and we had three more days to go. Day One had been quite fun and now we were winding down before turning in for the night.

One of the facilitators was a chap called, well let's call him Tony. Part of the course had involved interviewing him that afternoon and it was hard not to like him. Next to his free spirit, we were all control freaks. Our pressurised existences contrasted with his easy-paced seminar style and when he said he thoroughly enjoyed what he did for a living, we tended to envy rather than doubt him.

And now here we were. He had his pint and – you're not interested in what I was drinking. Later, maybe. The chat turned to the one book we all have in us and I asked Tony whether there was a topic he really wanted to tackle. He didn't have to think about it at all. There was. He thought he could write a book on leadership. He thought it an important topic, and he thought he had an angle on it that might help out. I have no doubt he could write the book and find the angle.

The question that occurred to me next was one I didn't get around to asking. I should have asked it. Any manual on evangelism would have mandated it. However, I didn't, and I regret it. But I can't recreate the chat on the barstool. Somehow, it didn't seem to fit with the late evening ambience to ask him whether he had taken a look at Jesus' leadership style.

And yet the question has grown on me. Not so much Jesus as a leader, but Jesus on leadership. Jesus training the next generation of leaders. Before small group workshops were invented, Jesus picks twelve people out of the crowd and invests a few years in them. Before the manuals on self-discovery had started to pile up, Jesus is willing to let his followers find out what they are really like, faithfully returning to pick up the pieces and to restore the battered image to a trueness it had never known.

Then there is the teaching. While Jesus will let his students try and fail, he is not prepared to let them develop simply by regurgitating themselves. Self-discovery is part of the package but there is serious element of teaching. Again, Jesus is master of the question that draws people out. His teaching has that passive angle which relies on the student coming back for more, but there is much of the didactic, of the challenging, even of the confrontational.

All the time, he has an agenda, throwing trickier and trickier problems into their laps, shielding them at first from the difficulties of ministry, then involving them, then working through the hardships with them and finally leaving them with the most impossible ministry of all. And they fulfil it.

The most amazing aspect of Jesus' approach to leadership training is how well it worked. Eleven out of twelve passed the course and went on to turn the world upside down.

My training course turned out to be tough. It was one of those encounters with yourself which is both painful and stilling, where you leave a little raw but very content and at ease. Over the following year or so, I've thought a lot about how we work with other people. How we get the best out of one another. How we learn to lead. My secular experience has resonated with contributions from other Christians – Rob Parsons' *Sixty Minute Father*, and Roy Clements' *Strength of Weakness*.

There must be thousands of Christian managers out there, like me, keeping their heads below the parapet. We take in a mix of excellent, mediocre and even dangerous seminars on leadership and rarely try to see where it fits with the faith or whether what works in the workplace has any place in the church. I realise that we run a risk of seeing Jesus' ministry in the light of our latest discovery. I hope we can spot the danger and clear it. But it may be that some of the insights of our age work because they have glimpsed a real truth. Where it is real, important and timeless, we can be sure that Jesus will have known about it and applied it, skilfully, confidently, and so perceptively that those watching will hardly have been aware of it.

Without wishing to excuse my lack of courage, there is a sense in which getting Tony to take on a book like this would have been the easy way out. I have no doubt it would have done wonderful things for Tony. But sometimes you have to sit down and follow your own vision. Nothing I can write or you can read will make Jesus any more wonderful or masterful than he really is. However, in watching someone do something that you have tried and stumbled at, you can get an exciting sense of what a terrific person it takes to do the job properly. I hope the trail leads you to that fresh sense of wonder in the presence of Jesus.

Two more things and the preface is over. Mine was a Pepsi. And thank you, Tony, wherever you are.

Introduction

Is this just another book on training?

I hope not! It is certainly not a book about training pastors or ministers. In fact, the people with most exposure to the training I am looking at may not be conventional church leaders at all. Nor is it a book about how to run Bible studies, although you might get some ideas here. It is not even about setting up a training programme in your church – although I hope it will help a lot if you are doing that.

So what is this book about?

Well, it is about the sort of training that many Christians get today through their careers in secular work. It is about trying to see whether the courses paid for by our employers have any value in Christian service. This, of course, creates a slight conundrum because Christians who go on such courses are not the ones you might typically think of as trainers in a church setting. Conversely, the 'professional' Christians tend not to receive on-the-job training from secular employers. For me, the answer to this little riddle lies in everyone having a ministry and therefore having something to pass on to a successor. There are other ways around the apparent disconnect and I hope the best ones for your situation will occur to you as you read the book.

In terms of training methods, this book is also about the way Jesus trained his disciples and the parallels we might identify between his methods and some modern management training.

Pulling this all together, I hope you will find three things in this book that provide a slightly different angle on Christian ministry and training. These themes can be woven into something that links service and training. If you are still trying to decide whether this book is worth reading, here they are.

Secular training and Christian service

I am pretty sure that this is not the most important strand, but it was my way into this material and so perhaps we can start here. By secular training I am thinking about the courses people are sent on that cover 'soft skills'. As well as technical training (such as how to operate a piece of machinery or use a spreadsheet), many people find themselves on such courses as how to conduct interviews; how to prepare for retirement; how to assess and motivate team members; how to negotiate; how to manage change; and so forth. The list is a long one but I am sure you have the idea. In order that the training might provide lasting benefit, it sometimes comes in the form of a package, requiring preparation beforehand, some formal teaching and interactive sessions (at a training centre, perhaps) with a follow-up project or period of assessment back in the working environment. Often you are put in a team of 2-10 people who learn with you and help to assess progress.

I often wonder why so little of this seems to be applied to Christian service today. We have already alluded to part of the difficulty. Almost by definition, the vast majority of these courses have been given to people who are not 'professional' Christians. I am not saying that 'professional' Christians, such as your youth worker, vicar or even music director, may not have had such training. My guess is, however, that their training will have been less well funded and their opportunities to keep up-to-date will have been harder to come by. Another obvious reason is that we tend to draw a line between work and church. We tend to use those tools for work that have been paid for by work, and to get on with our Christian service (running the youth group, Christian summer camp, or whatever) as best we can.

Is there some way to lever this 'free' training into our Christian service? Did Jesus ever exploit the 'free' training of those who followed him?

Succession as part of a ministry

Secondly, I notice that training itself was high on Jesus' agenda. Jesus was not unique in having disciples – John the Baptist had disciples (e.g. Matt 11:2) – nor in appointing those who would carry the ministry on afterwards. For instance, Elijah appointed Elisha as his successor (1 Kings 19:19-21). So what is new here?

I think it is worth noting how much of his time the Master invests in the disciples. In fact, his entire public ministry is carried out with those who will carry it on.

Again I find myself asking why we seldom see this emphasis today. Today we tend to have stand-alone ministry. When our elders or deacons reach the end of a successful ministry, we look around for replacements. As we see from Samuel, this can also be a scriptural model. Some people are not replaced in that one-to-one sense. In the church, as in many other spheres of life, we recognise the impact of the giant who stands apart from the crowd, reaches astonishing goals and afterwards leaves a gaping hole that no-one else can fill.

The irony is that if anyone could claim to be irreplaceable it was Jesus. His work in salvation, atonement, and in opening up a new era in the relationship between God and man was and is entirely unique. No one could touch that and, fortunately, it will never need replication. And yet Jesus devotes an amazing amount of time to working with a group of disciples to whom he will entrust the next phase of the plan. I believe the gospels present us with a model of ministry and training that we may have missed because we have not been looking for it: selecting and training a successor to continue the task. Perhaps we could go even further and say that the real model here is to disciple with a view to filling the slot many times over. Our aim in Christian service is often to secure conversions, or perhaps to disciple converts through to maturity. The gospels give us a glimpse of a way to replicate our own ministry over and over again.

Jesus' training methods

Finally, in trying to piece this together, I have become conscious of how many of the methods Jesus used are around today, not necessarily in seminaries, Bible colleges or even at weekend leadership events, but in the hands of secular trainers whose job is to make the most of the human resources a company possesses. The emphasis on workshops, small groups, and the recognition of the role a mentor can play: these are typically reflected in the way Jesus sets out to train the fishermen who followed him.

Clearly we must be careful here. It is all too easy to try and fit Jesus into a management straightjacket of our own making. I hope this book does not do that. But if we see a pattern of training that is popular today and has a pedigree stretching back a couple of millennia – so much the better. It will also give us confidence to apply and experiment with these ideas.

So how are these themes developed?

In circulating various chapters, I have had some helpful criticism and I realise that it fits with other things I have written. I like to be surprised when I read but I think most people want to see where they are going. If you like surprises, skip to chapter 1 and commit yourself to reading the rest. If you like to get the big picture first, I will try to explain how the themes develop in the book.

There is a second reason for unwrapping this. Most of my working life has been involved in innovation of one sort or another. It is actually quite hard to work out, when you think you are onto something new, just exactly what is novel about it. I had a colleague once for whom this was a real issue. He would spend ages working through material that you could find in a standard text, and pass over deep insights in a sentence or two. I hope this chance to slow down and piece the themes together will help to make it clearer if there really are any new angles in this book and, if there are, where you might find them.

Starting at the beginning

Wasn't it the Jesuits who said, 'Give me the child 'til he be seven, and I'll give you the man'? And so I began by looking away from the world of work to the background training. My parents were missionaries but I have only recently begun to appreciate the massive benefits that accrue from such an upbringing. I hope that the material in the first chapter may help in two ways. Firstly, by highlighting the importance of consistent teaching throughout childhood, I hope it will encourage those engaged in children's and young people's work to keep the emphasis on content. I am not an expert in this field, so the style is something you will have to find elsewhere. Secondly, I hope it will encourage parents to bring the Bible to their children and to see themselves as playing a key role in training Christian leaders. Apart from being fun, it is one of the most challenging ways of learning yourself.

Developing the theme

Focusing more on Jesus as mentor and teacher, there are two chapters (2 and 5) examining his approach from my perspective as an interested, but inexpert, observer of teaching methods. I guess it is obvious why we need to do this and I trust it gives you a chance to bring your own expertise to bear. You will probably be able to glean insights from where you stand that my perspective will have obscured. Interspersed are a couple of chapters on the sort of techniques and training that we may learn through work – a chapter on questioning techniques (4) and one on secular training itself with some practical examples of how the techniques may be applied in a church context (3).

The rest of the book seeks to pull the lessons together, bringing some practical propositions out of the mix of ideas and examples. By that stage the basic ideas should be clearer. Finally, there is a challenge to take the blessings of training that we have received and to do something useful with them.

So who is this book aimed at?

I guess these ideas will work best in churches where everyone does something and therefore has something to pass on. A church where everyone is working and happy to work themselves out of a job provides maximum scope for using the assortment of skills and training gleaned from whatever opportunities we have had. It also provides the greatest opportunity to take someone under your wing and teach them what it is you are up to, why you enjoy the task and what your aspirations for it are.

In that sense it isn't targeted just at leaders in the conventional sense of the word. Many of the mentors might not yet recognise themselves as such. If, as a result of reading this, more people step up to the task of doing something for Jesus and training a co-worker to take it over, I will be dead chuffed.

I guess, as a man, I will have most to offer to other men. I hope there is a challenge for men who are doing OK at work, who have the skills and training to make their own lives and the lives of their families around them that little bit nicer and more comfortable. I hope some will decide they could also apply those skills to an even more exciting goal.

As a final note, this manuscript has taken a while to write but

I have not attempted to correct the time scales. Something that may have been 'recent' when I first wrote it, may now be 'a while ago' – but I have not amended the text. The same applies to incidents involving my sons who have grown since the stories were first committed to paper.

Enjoy…

1

Qualifications and Selection

It may not hold out much promise as an exciting start to the book, but we have to get as far back into the process as we can. Jesus didn't run a Sabbath school from which he recruited his disciples. He started with people, some of whom had already lived most of their lives, most of whom were past that mental malleability that makes learning a joy. He started with grown men. Clearly, he chose them. So what was he looking for?

When we start to ask these questions, there are two dangers. Firstly, we see Jesus so much as the Son of God that we give up any attempt to explain what he was up to in human terms. We have a picture of Jesus' ministry so focused on prayer and communion with his Father God that there is little room for personal planning or decision making. There is no point in trying to find a method because it was all worked out in heaven with foresight and omniscience. We are left, therefore, either to explore the same 'short circuit' to planning for ourselves, or to find completely different methods. I believe that either alternative will lead us to an impoverished style of leadership in the end.

A second danger lies in appreciating Jesus' humanity at the expense of his deity. This is the danger I mentioned in the introduction. We see Jesus purely in human terms: Jesus as a great teacher, Jesus as a revolutionary, Jesus as a management consultant. This approach has its rewards. For instance, Jesus was a magnificent teacher. Even through the ears and translations of others, the parables reach us with pace, colour, focus and that teasing flick at the end which separates the master narrator from lesser storytellers. To appreciate Jesus' excellence in his field is well worth the effort. But without any supernatural dimension we will fail to understand what is going on, and ultimately our own lives will be exposed as a cheap imitation of the original.

When scripture reveals truths to us that we find mutually exclusive, it is generally safer to embrace the extremes than to try to avoid them. So let's be aware of the pitfalls, appreciate the spiritual and miraculous side to Jesus' incomprehensible person but press on in hope that there might be methods that we can grasp and apply, too. So what was Jesus looking for when he chose his disciples?

Our first response is that he was not after qualifications. Matthew is perhaps the only one whom we would expect to find in possession of a degree – something in business administration, maybe. I do not know the Jewish educational system at the turn of the dating system in any detail but I suspect we're talking NVQs rather than GSCEs, A levels or degrees. In any case it won't help us with the question of qualifications.

Background training

If we try to guess at Jesus' selection criteria by asking what sort of things the successful candidates had in common, the most striking features are that they were all Jews and most of them were doing something else at the time.

And being Jewish did mean something academic. It meant knowing your Old Testament like the back of your hand. Their facility in quoting the Old Testament, whether it meant throwing a few stanzas of Joel into the most hair-raising maiden message of your life, or stirring a liberal mix of Isaiah into your correspondence, these men knew their scriptures.

I am just finishing a stint in Jeremiah, discovering again how his heart is torn apart by the unfaithfulness of God's people. The nation had forgotten God's law, was chasing every sexy idol it could lay its eyes on and the result was apostasy, cruelty, exploitation and, Jeremiah foresees, the judgment of God. Before Jeremiah had started preaching, God's law had almost been lost to the nation. After several years of Jeremiah's ministry, while they were undertaking a spot of heritage work in the Temple, a scroll containing the Law of Moses came to light. Its impact on the young monarch, Josiah, was startling and a reformation followed. In the end, however, the other gods won out in the fight for Jewish affections, people lost any appetite for God's law and the nation was deported to Babylon in a horrifying act of divine judgment.

In the middle of all of this, Jeremiah foresees a time when God's law will become part of the people (Jer 31:31-40), inscribed indelibly inside. Babylon settled the question of idols for the Jews forever. The chastened people repatriated under Cyrus knew the importance of scripture, and the system of synagogues that emerged was one of the great developments of post-exilic Judaism. It was also the system that turned out every candidate that Jesus selected.

Disciples v. Pharisees

We are wary today lest too much learning impinge on our faith. When we think 'synagogue', we think 'Pharisee' rather than 'disciple'. We remember that Jesus' most stinging criticism was levelled at those who could see no further than a framework of regulations. We recoil from a faith that is all head and no heart, recalling something about a letter which kills while the Spirit gives life (2 Cor 3:6).

And rightly so. But let's not confuse the disciples' schooling with Pharisaic sophistry or even with our own generation's preoccupation with education. With the possible exception of John, the disciples come across as ordinary, bright people with a sound, systematic training behind them. (Paul was well schooled and an academic, but most of the people whom God used to build the early church were thoroughly trained but not particularly intellectual.)

Through the systematic teaching of scripture to the nation, God was beginning to fulfil what he had promised, 'I will put my law in their minds and write it on their hearts.' (Jer 31:33). And when Jesus comes, the nation is prepared, with scripture burned deeply into its memory banks. And it was candidates with that kind of scriptural recall who went on to write our New Testament.

A cursory look at the disciples reveals an unexpected catholicity, embracing both a collaborator and a nationalist, with perhaps a preference for northerners and fishing. What we tend to miss is the enormous importance of all that training which was the birthright of every Jewish boy at the time, and which Jesus was able to pick up and use.

A Christian upbringing

So what are the implications for us? Well, firstly, thank God if you have had a sound Christian upbringing. Although Timothy's upbringing had been in a culturally mixed home, his Jewish mother and grandmother had taught him the scriptures, 'from infancy' (2 Tim 3:14,15). If you read Paul's correspondence with Timothy, you can see the impact his upbringing has had on his current ministry as a leader.

Let's not get this important point the wrong way around. We do not learn from Jesus that anyone who knows nothing of scripture until conversion as an adult cannot become a Christian leader. One of the most inspiring speakers I have come across locally has been a Christian for fewer than ten years and has exercised a county-wide ministry for much of that time. God is no more restricted by our background than he is by anything else. God is God and can work with anybody, preferring nobodies on the whole.

However, the message for us in leadership training is clearly to take responsibility for our children and young people and to ensure that they grow familiar with their Bibles, starting early. Doesn't all this smack of indoctrination? Well the word certainly conveys the idea of getting teaching inside someone. But I am not suggesting scripture to the exclusion of all else. My Mom, in particular, read to us as kids and I believe that reading to your children is very important. There are all kinds of wonderful books on the market today and part of the fun of being a modern parent is to discover them and enjoy them with your family. And as part of that diet of words and jokes, and sad stories, prose and, I hope, some poems, there needs to be priority on reading them Bible stories and even the Bible itself.

The Bible for children

Apart from anything else, it's fun. My children are six, four and one. All boys – we haven't worked out how to do girls. Reading the Bible with my elder two is one of the most stimulating things I do. Not every time, of course, and you have to learn to mix it up. But the Good News Bible is wonderfully accessible for Little People.

I managed to persuade my company to send me on a speed-reading course a few years ago. It was a great couple of days, some of the best value for money I never spent, and was delivered by the chap who had written the training material. The course rescued me from the slavery of believing I had to read every word to feel that I had mastered a document. Sometimes the index will tell you all you need to know on the subject. Sometimes you will have to read one passage a dozen times to master it. But you can be in control of your reading.

I am catching on that the same applies in reading the Bible to my kids. A little common sense will soon teach you when to skip on a few paragraphs, either because little minds are struggling with the plot or else because the material won't work for them yet. At other times, you need to stick with the story and ask some questions. Sometimes you just want to know if they have understood the facts. Other times you will discover that they understand what it is all about. I'm not an expert. I'm only here to report that, as well as being important, it's not that difficult and is extremely rewarding.

And it is rewarding. Last night we skipped Jesus' teaching on divorce (Matt 19:1-12) and read the story of the rich young man (Matt 19:16-30) which concludes with the mysterious statement, 'But many who are first will be last, and many who are last will be first.' Up piped a little voice. 'Was that like the meal where we were told the last would be first?'

I had forgotten that at a recent church lunch, one of the leaders had stood up halfway through to announce that the second course was ready and with true Christian fairness, he suggested that the tables went up in reverse order, offering a free translation of this proverb by way of explanation. And then we remembered that there had been more firsting and lasting because all the youngsters had woven their way up the queues, collected and devoured their meals, and had been caught at the front again before many of the grown-ups had had their first helping.

Is Jesus saying anything about grown-ups with empty plates at the front of the queue while the kids are sneaking in for seconds? Granted, that wasn't the original context, but you give me a better contemporary illustration of the adage. I find a freshness in children's ability to remember and throw the bits together and a challenge in trying to make sense in response. Again, it's going to be tricky and I don't expect to be able to give my boys a completely logical interpretation of all the pieces of truth they recall and try to fit together. But I have a great faith in the word itself. It will linger when I have passed on and will make sense in their lives long after my ideas have ceased to be relevant.

But, you say, I couldn't feel natural reading the Bible to my children. We don't interact that way. I don't ask them questions about what we have talked about. It just isn't me. One solution is to find a way of building the Bible into their lives in a way with which you can cope. However, this business of feeling natural may be a bit of a blind. Remember that first driving lesson? Did anything feel remotely natural or intuitive about it? Remember trying to get a feel for the pedals or forgetting all about the indicators while you braced yourself for another wild experiment in understeer? I guess almost anything new will start out as an unnatural experience and the trick is to learn as you go along and not to be too afraid of failure. Most children will flag it up when they are bored, and if they are enjoying themselves you won't be in any doubt for long.

Where do I fit in?

So is Christian leadership training only for Christian parents? I don't think so. I suspect that there is something there for Sunday school teachers and others involved with young people. I have to confess that I have never taught a Sunday school class, or been systematically involved with young people for well over a decade, so I haven't anything to offer there. My only plea would be to get plenty of content into your talks. In speaking locally, I sometimes catch sight of the material being targeted at a younger audience. Though wonderfully imaginative in terms of communication technique and approach, I do worry about undernourishment in the long term. I suspect that, sooner or later, we have to trust that God's word will make its own impact in lives, and just concentrate on delivering an effective dose.

So how about the rest? Well let's look around. Are there any rich people in the congregation? I believe wealth is a largely untapped resource that God gives us in the church. One of the great ways to get young people to do something is to offer prizes. Prizes that people would really want. Prizes that cost money. I memorised the order of the books of the New Testament because someone was running a competition. I read the New Testament through as a ten-year-old at five chapters a night because someone promised me a prize (and because my parents were wonderfully forbearing, preferring to ease up on bedtime principles in pursuit of a longer term agenda: I never remembered my readings until bedtime). Having gotten some momentum, inertia carried me on through the Old Testament, which I got through by the time I was twelve.

When did you last sponsor a competition in your church? We tried it some years ago and a few people rose to the challenge and have read their New Testament through. We even had a very little person claiming (and winning) a prize because she had read her Bible Story Book through. I guess we could have been more systematic about it all and should have repeated the exercise several times by now, but at least we can report that modern teenagers can compete in the reading stakes with anyone else. Want to pay for prizes? Think of it as a long-term investment.

And there are so many other ways God can use you, your resources, your family, your imagination, your whatever, to train leaders of the future by getting God's word into their minds and hearts. Once it is there, there is no limit to what the Holy Spirit can do with it.

So Jesus invests his very limited resource of time into people who have already been well trained. It makes sense. He also goes after people who are doing something else. Why? Was it because people who are busy in their career have an added dimension to their training? Or is Jesus averse to selecting the theologically trained? I cannot see the latter in the light of God's achievements through Paul, and church history bears ample witness to the powerful effect of a godly life allied to deep doctrinal insight.

Leaving and giving

We do not know what Philip was called away from or much about Nathaniel (aka Bartholomew?) (John 1:43-51) and details are sketchy about five of the others. However, the dramatic call to the brothers Peter and Andrew and also to James and John away from the family business is one of the exciting developments in Jesus' early ministry (Matt 4:18-22; Mark 1:14-20). Adding in Luke's account (Luke 5:1-11) and John's background (John 1:35-42), we get the impression that Jesus had prepared the path but the call, when it comes, clearly ushers in a new career. Jesus calls Matthew (aka Levi) from his desk at work (Matt 9:9-13; Mark 2:13-17; Luke 5:27-32). In all five cases, Luke tells us, they 'left everything and followed him'.

Many years later, John gives us a peek into heaven where we see 24 elders worshipping and their worship consists, in part, of laying down their crowns (Rev 4:9-11). All the way through scripture our worship consists in part of having something to give, from Abel (Gen 4:3-16) through the elaborate sequences of offerings described, for instance, in Numbers 7, to Mary with her pint of pure nard (John 12:1-8). Here, in the end of all time, people are still giving. It is a picture that helps me to make sense of the two conflicting insights we have of heaven, namely that it is a place of equality and of reward. If you all give your reward away, you are all equal.

And Jesus offers his would-be disciples the chance to share in that experience while they are still locked in time. As they walk away from the booth or the boats they, too, are giving – or in their case, giving up. Perhaps one of the greatest difficulties in training high quality leadership today is a shortage of people prepared to walk away from their brightest opportunities.

I doubt if I will be able to express this properly, but there is a sense in which the act of giving up is worthwhile in its own right. Even without their training in the University of Life, even without the transferable skills, even without all the benefits that accrue from having served a human master before they decide to serve the Lord, the fact that they have something to give up adds content to their worship and quality to their leadership potential.

For some it means walking away once and for all, rather like the disciples. Mark, in particular, indicates the security James and John left behind, since their father, Zebedee, was sufficiently well off to have hired hands. For others it may mean walking away day after day as they realise that they cannot excel at work and be the leader God is calling them to be. While my parents took the former course, it is the latter with which I struggle. Renouncing ambition while working your hardest to do well and to push things forward at work is hard for me, and it has taken God a long time to blunt the edge of my appetite here. But he is doing what he set out to do.

Maybe one day I'll be able to write something which does justice to the call but for now we note that Jesus is looking for people with the devotion and confidence to walk away. 'No-one who puts his hand to the plough and looks back is fit for service in the kingdom of God' (Luke 9:62).

Survival skills

Jesus is not explicit in his reasons for choosing people who were already trained or training in something else. It makes good sense to choose people who are well adjusted and able to survive a working environment. Paul uses a similar argument to Timothy: 'If anyone does not know how to manage his own family, how can he take care of God's church?' (1 Tim 3:5).

While a few people come to Jesus to sort out their domestic arrangements (Luke 10:38-42; 12:13), there is absolutely no evidence that Jesus invested any of his time with his disciples in such areas as marriage counselling or debt management, although he does have to put time into their relationships with one another. If one aspect of good leadership is picking winners, Jesus has chosen a team of well balanced people who will not distract him with a plethora of problems they should have learned to sort out for themselves.

If that sounds harsh in an age where life is so much more complicated and pressures on our purses and personalities are extreme, it is worth looking around our churches and asking where the brightest of our brains, the most pleasing of our personalities, the most creative of our talents, the fairest of our congregations, and the most energetic of our workers are investing their talents. By and large, those who can look after themselves are doing so – and very nicely thank you. It is hard to believe that God's kingdom would not explode if these talents were suddenly and selflessly channelled into his service.

Against the truth that congregations should offer their best people to God is the truth for the individual that God's strength is made perfect in weakness (2 Cor 12:7-10) and God produces some of the most spectacular results using the most unlikely resources. However in his leadership selection, as a general rule, Jesus seems to be fairly hard nosed – the course will not be a doddle.

Thinking it through

1. In the light of Jesus' selection criteria, how would you set a syllabus for your Sunday school?
2. What were the last ten books you read to your children? Now what will the next ten be?

3. Skim John's Gospel picking up themes around 'knowing'. To what extent is John's concept of knowing fact-based and how much is personal knowledge?

4. You have been put on the selection committee for your local pastor: list 5 areas of background you would like to explore – and plan the opening question for each (chapter 4 might help you with ideas on framing the questions).

5. A recently converted couple approach you offering to put £250 a year into children's work at your church. What plans would you make?

6. A recently converted teenager feels God's call to full-time service. You are asked for your advice. How would you respond?

7. Your church is supporting a young family at Bible college with a view to church planting. They come to you when they are seriously in debt and with consequential marital tensions. What plans might you explore with them?

2

Jesus as Mentor

'Come, follow me', says Jesus at the start of his earthly ministry (Matt 4:19, etc). Peter heard and responded. He hears the same call after the resurrection (John 21:19): 'Follow me!' Your concordance will help you trace the number of times in between those two events that Jesus issues the call. Years later, when writing to struggling churches, Peter presents Jesus as the supreme example, reminding them of his suffering so 'that you should follow in his steps' (1 Pet 2:21b).

Jesus' self-awareness, sense of mission and focus on his own role sit so unnaturally beside his generous, sacrificial and self-giving life. In fact many people have noted that, unless he is fully God and fully man, unless the explanation for his existence is the mind-blowing, magnificent explanation that the early disciples took to the ends of the earth, there is something horribly flawed about him. The mad, bad or God argument draws heavily on this evidence.

It is not simply that people played up the exemplary side of his character at the time, or afterwards. Everywhere we examine the story, we find an innate understanding that he is there to be followed: 'I am the light of the world. Whoever follows me will never walk in darkness but will have the light of life' (John 8:12). Nowhere is Jesus more explicit about his role as mentor than after he has washed the disciples' feet (John 13:2-17): 'Do you understand what I have done for you? … I have set you an example that you should do as I have done for you.' A few days later, after his death and resurrection, Jesus is handing on the baton (John 20:21), 'As the Father has sent me, I am sending you.'

And the disciples stepped up to this challenge, not just to follow Jesus but to take up the responsibility of being examples. Paul is explicit: 'Follow my example as I follow the example of Christ' (1 Cor 11:1). We discover that the church at Thessalonica did just that (1 Thess 1:6). In their turn, these early leaders passed the mentor's baton on, too. Peter writes to a group of early church leaders and encourages them to be 'examples to the flock' (1 Pet 5:3). To Timothy, Paul says, 'And the things you have heard me say in the presence of many witnesses entrust to reliable men who will also be able to teach others' (2 Tim 2:2).

To our society, knee-deep in manuals, instructions, legislation, guidelines, codes of practice, reportage, textbooks and other verbiage, Jesus is an amazing character. He does not think it necessary to write anything down for his followers: no special scroll, crib sheet for crucial situations, or book of beliefs. Instead, he chooses a few groups of people and introduces them to the most inspiring and effective on-the-job training imaginable.

We are familiar with the twelve disciples and note within that group a select three in Peter, James and John, often admitted to training sessions from which the rest are excluded. There is also a group of women (Mark 15:40,41) and a group of six dozen (Luke 10:1), while Luke numbers the embryonic church at about 120 people (Acts 1:15). The picture we are left with is of a well-defined school of disciples that Jesus works with consistently, while he works and interacts with other groups, too, including the ever present, and pressing, crowds.

So what does Jesus do with these people? What will they learn on the road with him, in the synagogues, by the seaside, that they never learnt from their local rabbis? How will he equip them in a few years with the power, tools and experience to make the gospel stick? How will they take it beyond the peasants of Galilee, to Jewish rulers, to foreigners, into all kinds of cultural contexts, to officials at every level, and to the heart of the Empire – to Rome itself?

Personal example

Who is your spiritual mentor? There must be someone whose life has had an impact on yours, someone you look up to, respect, admire, or just like to turn over the odd tricky problem with. I guess for me it was my Dad. He wasn't the sort of Dad you wanted to discuss everything with – the Dad-as-a-Pal I would sometimes have liked him to be. In many ways, my Mom fulfilled that role and we saw a great deal more of her. But he taught me many of the basic lessons about being a Christian. He taught me about getting up early and having a quiet time before the rest of the day got in the way. He taught that to me not by telling me or preaching it to others (although he did that, too), but by doing it. There must have been hundreds of mornings that I would come downstairs to find him reading his Bible in a chair by the fire or kneeling there in prayer.

He taught me that you pray about things when life gets hairy. And things did get hairy. As faith missionaries, my parents did not have a salary from their mission but would trust God for their income. Whatever was sent in for them would be forwarded. I can remember many times growing up when the remittance would come in late, or turn out to be a lot less than would be needed. And they would both trust God, cheerfully and prayerfully and in faith – and we always made it through the month.

He taught me that you have to know your Bible if you are going to get anything out of it worth giving to others. He would study and meditate – not because he felt he had to, but because he would get taken up with it. Many times it was all he wanted to talk about. My Dad could be very frustrating. But he had a great God whom he trusted implicitly and he taught me that that was worth any amount of anything else.

So who is your mentor? What have you learned from them? What do you hope to learn?

Prayer

What did the disciples learn from their mentor? One day Jesus is praying. The disciples wait until he has finished and then they ask him to teach them to pray like that, too (Luke 11:1-4). Why? Why would a group of grown men ask Jesus to teach them to pray? Were Jesus' prayers such a contrast to their own that they wanted his? Was it because they recognised prayer as one of the things that their Rabbi could, and should teach them? Was it that, like us, they found prayer really difficult, and saw that Jesus' prayer life was so effective that they had to have it?

Apart from Peter's wanting to walk on the water with Jesus (Matt 14:22-36), we do not find too many such requests. It is interesting that they never wanted to practise walking on the water again, nor did they ask to be able to perform miracles, although they did try – and failed – to copy Jesus in healing someone's son (Mark 9:14-29). But it is the prayer that Jesus taught which was carefully remembered and passed down to us. For some reason Jesus' prayer life made an impression.

Was it because Jesus linked a lack of prayer with their failure to heal the boy in Mark 9? Was it the raw sincerity when 'he offered up prayers and petitions with loud cries and tears... and was heard because of his reverent submission' (Heb 5:7)? Was it the time he would make for prayer in the deep dusk before dawn, trudging out to find somewhere to be alone (Mark 1:35)? Was it the sheer intensity of those last prayers in Gethsemane?

However it was, these curious, watching fishermen soon linked the fact that Jesus was different with the way he prayed. And the way he prayed made them want to pray. I know lots of people who make me feel guilty for the way I pray. There are people through whom I see how important prayer is. But there are not many people whose prayers make me want to pray – to pray or burst.

Our toddler is just at the talk-or-burst stage. He so wants to talk, but his word box is still pretty empty. Every now and then his need to talk goes way beyond his ability to articulate and so he just inarticulates. He jabbers away like crazy, with all the right expressions, and you know how badly he needs to say something, to interact, to breathe the rich air of conversation. One day, of course, he will. Do I have that sort of drive to pray?

Survival training

And so this band of fishermen comes to Jesus. They have to learn to pray as he prays. Perhaps they gained the impression that Jesus' prayer life was about survival rather than duty. He longed to be in his Father's presence, longed to get away from the crowd to recharge and find direction. Maybe in our society, stifled with sound, suffocated with views and opinion, driven by forces friendly, fearsome and fanatical, there is a lesson for us from Jesus. Secular movements recognise the need and try to fill it with focus or meditation. Many give up altogether and throw themselves into the noisy, haphazard tide of busy lives.

Every so often, my wife and I find ourselves talking our way through the week past. Usually it is Sunday evening, with the kids in bed, the house quiet, and a busy weekend behind us. Sometimes, having talked, we decide to pray together. I would love to say that we pray for hours but we don't. We pray, usually turn about, until we have worked through the things that bothered us. And something does happen. We start in desperation and we finish with a sense of peace. Sometimes we are overwhelmed when we begin and we are quietly confident when we conclude. Thinking back over those times, I get some insight into why prayer was such a matter of survival to Jesus.

Naturally speaking

If Jesus' prayer life left an impression on his followers because it was essential or sincere, they were also aware of how natural it was. Jesus is happy to give thanks in public as he blesses the loaves and fish. There are also the little prayers, born out of sheer happiness or need. The disciples had returned, overjoyed from a big mission, and Jesus is delighted with what God is doing (Luke 10:21,22). The result? A short shaft of praise. He prays a very public (and brief!) prayer of praise before he splashes back the tide of death and calls Lazarus to live again (John 11:41,42). In John 12:28 ('Father, glorify your name!') the prayer is even briefer and very closely interwoven with the conversation. You saw the same pattern in Luke 10:21,22 where Jesus' prayer and commentary are very hard to disentangle. If Jesus' example taught them that prayer was something apart from the rough and tumble of daily life, an essential underpinning, his life of prayer also taught them that it had to be woven into it.

I guess we need to build these short prayers into everything. When we are stirred, inexplicably happy, when something we have prayed for is finally achieved, how about those little rivets of praise which fasten heaven and earth together for a second or two around you?

Have you been out driving at night with a full moon painting the countryside a soft silver, etching the clouds in delicate relief from the deep backdrop of sky? At times like that do you give a yelp of happiness and say thanks to your Heavenly Father? He paints glorious skies every day. He is wasteful with his beauty. There are clouds that people have never sat on – and it is beautiful from there. There are deserted mountaintops from which the sunset views are awesome. For a world flooded with thrilling, prodigal beauty, we ought to say thanks, at least on the odd occasions when it stirs our own souls. It is so good for us and it helps to stitch together our expectations of heaven and our appreciation of earth.

Another way of weaving prayer into everyday existence: I heard of a chap who, when people came up and asked him to pray for them, would stand there and pray for them. The person who told me the story noted that it tended to sort out the serious from the synthetic. I find it is generally appreciated. Someone has just shared something with you that has been a source of hurt or worry. On the spot prayers can be specific and well-informed while everything is fresh in your mind. And people know that something has been done. I give the practice ten out of ten.

The early chapters of Acts portray a group of people bursting readily into prayer. They had clearly ingested the teaching. Whether things have gone badly or well, they make it an opportunity to stitch some Psalms together and praise God for his greatness or for the opportunity he is giving them to identify with Jesus in suffering.

Prayer to survive on, sincere prayer, spontaneous prayer. How about structured prayer? Does structure worry you? Have you ever wondered about those ancient writings, many of which are rich with structure? I drift back to Psalm 34 – an acrostic. Clearly written from an ivory tower by someone with the time for the meticulous exercise of starting each line with a new letter of the alphabet. Except that the traditional ascription (and I'll run with a traditional ascription any time) is to David at a time of intense personal stress and danger. Perhaps cultures less reliant on written material than our own tend naturally toward more structured expression. After all, rhymes, mnemonics, verbal patterns and other tricks help you to remember the prayer, and with it the preceding precariousness, not to mention the deliverance that followed.

The Lord's Prayer is a model prayer – an elegantly simple framework for lots of other prayers. Perhaps it is in Jesus' prayer in John 17 that we best see the structure. Was this the whole prayer or has John picked and edited the highlights? I guess I am an innocent abroad, but I go for a tight structured prayer from the Master, perhaps even reported in its entirety. My experiences of trying to edit unstructured conversation into crisp minutes of the meeting have left me with a strong belief that structure emerges reluctantly from chaos. Even with word processors offering cut and paste, edit, try it, change it, and start to work on the next phrase – even with all that, firm structure can be elusive. But the structure of Jesus' prayer here goes well beyond firm. It is a fine, elegant, thoughtful piece of praying.

Two other things before we move on from John 17. My guess is that Jesus would have prepared this somehow. Most of us are so into spontaneity in prayer that we miss the most obvious interpretation that Jesus has prepared for this. Under what other circumstances would we assume that a conversation which opens, 'Father, the time has come' is anything other than a well-prepared response to a climactic event as it unfolds? Most of us prepare our talks, lessons and worship sessions at church. What preparation goes into our praying? The problem is not eased if we enjoy a liturgical form of worship, since real preparation with someone else's words is no easier than preparing our own.

Nor am I saying that all our prayers must be drilled into us. I am not even saying that Jesus had planned every word in sequence and then recited the prayer. With practice cadences can fall spontaneously into place within a planned structure. Not all our prayers need this kind of structure. What I am saying is that Jesus used structure at the time of his greatest need and there is evidence from the Psalms that others had found the same solution generations before.

I would also guess that this was not the first time Jesus had prayed like this. We have a strange belief that when we are really under pressure we will be able to perform in ways we have never done before. To an extent that is true: acts of heroism often involve feats of strength, speed or endurance, of which the individual had never imagined himself or herself capable. However, most of us revert to character rather than away from it under pressure. Any sergeant major will tell you that the way to get people to behave like heroes is to drill the basics into them. Make the procedure mundane and when the mind is numb, the heroic becomes the only way forward.

Wedding speeches are a good example of these two points. The best speeches come from those who have spoken in public before and have prepared well. The chap who has researched the groom's schooldays, or who has spent time recalling that first fishing trip where the fish stayed wet and everyone else got wet – that sort of chap tends to deliver the goods in the heat of the moment. The most forgivable speeches (and you cannot have a bad speech at a wedding) come from those who have underprepared and are out of practice, from people who keep putting off the speechwriting, hoping that a flash of inspiration generated in the heat of the moment will see them through.

Pulling it all together, we see that Jesus' life of prayer impressed his followers so much that they wanted to pray like he prayed. Jesus' prayer life was a sincere matter of survival. It was spontaneous. And finally, on the right occasion, it was structured. Were Jesus' prayers short? Certainly the examples of prayer overheard fit that category. Can you have short prayers in the extended settings in which Jesus often spent time with his Father? Maybe, maybe not. Perhaps it depends on how much talking you think you have to do when you are on your own with God.

And his disciples learned to pray. They praised and prayed, were filled with the Spirit and became bold (Acts 4:31). They prayed while they were martyred (Acts 7:60). The convincing evidence that Saul of Tarsus had been converted was that he was praying (Acts 9:11). They prayed the dead back to life (Acts 9:40) and prison doors opened in response to their prayers (Acts 12:1-17). In fact, in that last example of Peter's miraculous release from prison, they managed to pray beyond what they thought possible. And of course, good mentoring is like that, you pick up the lifestyle and are suddenly surprised by the results.

Practical sessions

Different disciplines treat practical sessions differently, but they are usually characterised by a cool breeze of reality. For me at university, it was laboratory based. You discovered basic things: the reason your circuit would not work was because you had forgotten to switch the power supply on. You began to put the teaching in context, and a mass of symbols, equations and concepts would begin to mean something as you looked at the untidy wire work before you or used a piece of equipment to make a measurement.

You shift into a new gear when you have to make it work in the real world. I can still remember the only time I have been in a Jensen. Sitting in the passenger seat, I remember the frustration of dawdling behind a lesser roadster hogging the outside lane. I remember slipping into the middle lane and being pressed into my seat at a speed already above the speed limit. On the job training is a bit like that.

I remember 'doing' crystallography in the lecture theatre. Almost everyone who tried to educate us in solid state physics started with the same incomprehensible equation. We all learned the equation and duly scored at exam time by reproducing it. We could explain what it meant and explain (sort of) why it was important. We also memorised (or failed to memorise) the standard crystal structures. I have to say I left without ever being inspired by crystallography. And then I went to work. I met a chap who could just look at crystalline material and tell you about it. He could see its structure and orientation. He could talk about its properties, what would happen if you applied a voltage from here to there, or how light would behave passing through it. Although I had most of the bits in my head when I went to work, nobody had told me that crystallography could be relevant, much less fun. And on the job I learnt how to design a few devices in certain crystals.

So how does on the job training work for the disciples? We find Jesus testing them in the crisis of several thousand hungry people (more than the five thousand in the title by which we recall the event). All four gospel writers (Matt 14:13-21; Mark 6:30-44; Luke 9:10-17; John 6:1-15) recall how Jesus threw the question back to the disciples: how would they feed the crowd? Afterwards, they recognised this as a practical test set by Jesus to his team of students – a sort of group examination. A personal examination, too, since Philip seems to have been especially involved in the question. In at the deep end?

Why do teachers set almost impossible tests? Sometimes they are so good, that questions that daunt the students appear trivial to them. I remember a maths teacher who was teaching us integration and differentiation. They go together a bit like addition and subtraction do: if you add three to a number and then subtract three again, you end up where you started. If you integrate a function and then differentiate it, you get back to where you started. He would explain integration in terms of guessing the answer and then differentiating back to check your guess. Which was fair enough – except that his guesses were perceptive and mine were generally hopeless. I have to say that, after several more years of maths, I found that he was right – you got a good feel for the right guess.

So what is the gap between teacher and student here? Why does Jesus think feeding a crowd is a good start and why are the disciples unable to rise to the challenge? Is this miracle just a case of Jesus being so far ahead of his students that even something which he thinks is easy is, in fact, very difficult for them? There would seem to be something in this – although I have expressed the idea very inadequately. Jesus is certainly frustrated by his disciples' inability to take charge of the physical. He is mystified by their fear in the storm, 'Why are you still afraid? Do you still have no faith?' (Mark 4:40). In their turn, they are terrified by his total command over the storm (Mark 4:41). On another boat trip they are concerned because they have forgotten the provisions and, again, Jesus cannot understand their worry over material things. Material problems, in Jesus' view, are easily sorted. After going methodically through the feeding of the 4,000 and the 5,000 (Mark 8:14-21), Jesus asks, 'Do you still not understand?'

This, of course, fits with Jesus' teaching about not worrying over food, drink, or clothes (Matt 6:25-34). It is also consonant with his warning to fear the one with the power to throw into hell, rather than those who can only kill the body (Luke 12:4,5). A very little faith will transplant a mulberry tree into the sea, says Jesus (Luke 17:6). The same contrast between the temporal and eternal comes up when Jesus decides to forgive the paralytic's sins before healing him physically (Matt 9:1-8; Mark 2:1-11). The local experts thought they scented blasphemy – and to some extent their reaction was much better attuned to reality than ours. Our first priority would probably have been to heal the chap of his paralysis – and our generation would probably have regarded the offer of forgiven sins as incidental. By contrast, they realized that forgiving sin was an altogether more serious business than healing bodies. It is Jesus' question which brought this story to my mind: 'Which is easier: to say, "Your sins are forgiven," or to say, "Get up and walk"?' (Matt 9:5).

Well, which is easier? In the story we have just looked at, Jesus shows himself to be master of both. On the whole, we get the impression that, as far as Jesus was concerned, the physical, the visible, the temporal, was an easier proposition than the spiritual, the invisible, the eternal.

If the disciples were reluctant to take up the challenge and feed the crowd, we see the opposite difficulty when they try to heal an epileptic boy. Here they attempt something that is too difficult for them. All three synoptic writers indicate that there was also a spiritual dimension (Matt 17:14-23; Mark 9:14-29; Luke 9:37-43). It sounds as though the disciples, presented with the father's pleas, attempt and fail to deal with the situation. Once again, Jesus is disturbed at their lack of faith – see especially Matthew's account. However, when the disciples gather round to review the incident, Jesus indicates that the problem is a hard one, requiring prayer and, in some manuscripts, fasting.

Young chemistry students often want to get ahead of the course and precipitate wonderfully coloured salts from exotic chemicals, while the teacher wants them to grasp the basics of bonds or acid-base reactions. My kids want to build a robot for Robot Wars. Their teachers are convinced that learning to read and calculate is more important. Again, don't get me wrong, some of the most intuitive and clever electronics people I know find the academic side of the subject both boring and difficult. The point here is that a good mentor sets the right agenda, and keen students sometimes focus on what is interesting rather than what is important.

So problems that Jesus thinks it worth their while tackling, his trainees shrink away from, while they will have a go (and fail) at things which appear worthwhile to them but trickier in retrospect. Jesus never fails in anything physical which he attempts. Yet there are barriers of unbelief and of people's wills that Jesus is unable to overcome. And so we observe that the Master and his apprentices have a very different view of what is easy and what is hard.

We could turn to the relative importance of signs and wonders versus a lower profile ministry in prayer, teaching or evangelism as we seek to apply this to our generation. For those interested, there is a question at the end to ponder on.

There may, of course, have been another reason why Jesus takes his disciples by surprise. Sometimes going in at the deep end is the only way to get to grips with a topic. Sometimes, feeling scared and out of your depth is a risky but necessary side of the learning experience. In her nurse's training, my wife and her friends used to joke that, when it came to learning new procedures, you saw one, did one and then taught one.

Luke records at least two examples of Jesus sending out teams to do as he has done. The synoptic gospels report Jesus sending out the Twelve (Matt 10; Mark 6:6b-13,30; Luke 9:1-6,10) but only Luke gives us the second campaign with 70 or 72 (Luke 10:1-24). Luke's chronology is interesting in this respect, since feeding the crowd of more than 5,000 is sandwiched between the two. With the first campaign having been so successful, it is less difficult to see why Jesus should have tested them with a tricky problem.

A two-phase learning process with twelve and then 72 makes sense, since the disciples are able first to learn for themselves and then to be the old hands, with a new, wider selection of recruits. No special mention is made of the Twelve taking a lead in the second campaign, although they do receive an extra, private, debriefing afterwards (Luke 10:23,24).

Jesus' technique here consists of a briefing session covering both practical and spiritual matters, followed by the exercise itself. As far as we can tell, Jesus did not lead either campaign. Matthew indicates that, having commissioned the disciples, Jesus went elsewhere to teach and preach (Matt 11:1) while the reports in both cases indicate that the students returned with news to a Jesus who had not been with them. Afterwards with the Twelve, Jesus wants to get them away for rest and a chance to work through things with them. However he is frustrated in this, since the crowd will not leave them alone (see Luke 9:11), and indeed it is that very crowd which is miraculously fed in the end. With the larger group, Jesus gets a chance to talk it through but not to escape.

And again, we see that they learned the lessons, for Acts is full of people who knew how to preach and to heal. They knew how to plan and conduct evangelistic campaigns. They appreciated especially the spiritual dimension of the exercise (see Luke 10:18-20) and the need to be guided by the Holy Spirit.

So what are the lessons? It seems to work best with concise preparation in which Jesus sets out clear objectives and a plan of action. The practical is surprisingly light on supervision, and then Jesus comes in at the end to pick up and reinforce the important messages. A textbook approach. Only the textbooks were still centuries away.

We may be surprised by the brevity of the preparation and by Jesus' completely 'hands-off' style. However, we must remember that the disciples had already followed Jesus for a while (a few months? ...longer?). They had seen other campaigns and, presumably, listened to a great deal of teaching. Secondly, we have to remember that Jesus has chosen his disciples and they benefit from the basic training and qualifications described in chapter 1. Finally, they lived in a culture where this type of ministry was acceptable, perhaps even expected.

Clearly, one would need to modify the regime when dealing with a group of young people or brand new converts, or when addressing a wildly different social context. However, given our distance from the original events, the method looks remarkably robust.

Watch this

Good demonstrations are an art form. Whether the lecturer decides to stand on a trolley and propel himself or herself across the lecture theatre using fire extinguishers, or to burst a red balloon by shining a green laser at it, there will be times when you need to watch something that you may not be able to try at home.

Peter, James and John get selected for special treatment in this way. Why did Jesus choose to work with a few (one of whom would die an early martyr's death) in a special way? Is it part of a graded approach – deep training to a few, solid training to a few more and very broad-based training to a significant number? Is it just the time factor – you cannot train all of the people all of the time? Whatever the reason, and however the choice, we note that twelve people is a largish group to take everywhere. In retrospect, we also note that the two surviving members of the 'inner circle' had a major impact on the early church.

Peter, James and John observe events from which the others are excluded. Jairus' daughter (Matt 9:18-26; Mark 5:21-43; Luke 8:40-56) is an example. Luke notes that it was a small selection of disciples who actually went in and saw the girl raised to life.

Two other examples must have seared themselves into the minds of the three, although there was nothing to learn by way of technique. Jesus wants to burn some things into their brains, presumably because there will be much ahead to discourage them without this preparation. The transfiguration, where the three see Jesus in a very different light, is the first and the second is Gethsemane. All three synoptic gospels report the transfiguration (Matt 17:1-13; Mark 9:2-13; Luke 9:28-36). Perhaps

this was part of the recollection behind John's assertion, 'We
have seen his glory' (John 1:14). Peter is much more explicit in
recalling the event: 'We were eye-witnesses of his majesty…
when we were with him on the sacred mountain' (2 Peter 1:16-
18).

Jesus at prayer in his final hours is the other picture to sustain
the inner circle in its times of greatest need. Matthew and Mark
tell us explicitly that Peter, James and John went on with Jesus
(Matt 26:37; Mark 14:33). In this last example, we see what a
magnificent mentor Jesus really was. It is one thing to invite
your student in to watch a particularly intricate piece of surgery.
One can understand bringing a student along when your
research is noted and appreciated by someone really important.
But how many mentors would have their students there at times
of greatest need? It may be a tribute to his humanity that Jesus
needs human support at this time and is so deeply disappointed in his disciples as a result. Yet desperate circumstances come
to all of us, and Jesus wants his followers to know what to do
when they arrive.

You won't have time to give everyone all they need. You may
have time to give a few people some deep insights. Jesus teaches us the importance of offering a balanced set of experiences to
the few whom we have the privilege of guiding.

The Negative message

One of the great rules, you are told, of group learning is never
to undermine anyone's offering. Everyone has a contribution to
make. The worst thing you can do is to undermine a person's
self-confidence. While completely non-judgmental exercises can
be surprisingly rewarding and make for great learning, most
group teaching needs some steering and sometimes that means
saying no. The English are particularly unwilling to find ways
of saying no and can resort to stupendous subtlety in the art.
How does Jesus deal with the negative side of group learning?
Does he always affirm the opinions that his disciples proffer?

As we probably expect, Jesus has a range of approaches at his
disposal and he mixes his responses to suit the need. The most
shocking block Jesus puts on anyone's advice is that given to
Peter (Matt 16:23; Mark 8:33), 'Get behind me Satan!' It shocks
us that Jesus should use this terminology to one of his own dis-

ciples and to one of the inner circle. The language itself shocks us. I do not know how you come to terms with this passage, but there are some things we can learn from it.

For instance, there are life or death issues. Today we are so aware of people's feelings that we lose sight of the eternal land-scape behind. Perhaps it is a reaction to the days when we would fight for our view of the truth no matter who got hurt. There is a story floating around this area of someone who sent his daughter, I think it was, home from a church business meet-ing, because he did not want her to hear what he was about to say to someone else at the meeting. Harsh words are, sadly, all too common a feature of church business meetings. And we are right to react against that. But there are times when the issue is more important than the personalities.

I remember reading Francis Schaeffer's commentary on Joshua and noting how he commended the main body of Israelites because they were prepared to go to war, if necessary, with the Reubenites, the Gadites and half of the tribe of Man-asseh over their apparent apostasy (Josh 22). These people had all fought side by side to conquer the land and see God's prom-ises fulfilled in their lifetime. The smaller group that had asked for a settlement on the far side of the Jordan had returned in peace after the battles were over. And then they built what appeared to be an idolatrous altar. The other tribes were, quite literally up in arms. Here was something that counted for more than kindred or all the blood spilt in establishing a homeland. And they were right. Fortunately, they were wise as well as will-ing, and the delegation they sent across the Jordan established the facts before a conflict ensued.

If there are issues that transcend the personalities, the other thing to note is that there are not that many of them. Jesus never responds to a disciple like this again. This seems to be a once-in-a-lifetime occurrence.

That is not to say that Jesus does not put his foot down very clearly: 'Let the little children come to me, and do not hinder them…' (Matt 19:14; Mark 10:14). Jesus tells the disciples that they were wrong. And when John tells Jesus how he tried to stop a stranger casting out demons, Jesus tells him he was wrong (Mark 9:38-41; Luke 9:50).

At other times, Jesus seems to let the issue ride and picks it up again later. Remember the argument about who was the greatest (Mark 9:33-37; Luke 9:46-48)? Putting the two accounts together, we guess that Jesus was aware of the argument but had not been close enough to have heard for himself exactly what was being said. He knows, however, what the issue is. He opens it up, as we will come to expect, with a question, 'What were you arguing about on the road?' He fills the embarrassing silence with some teaching on leadership and servanthood along with a visual aid in the form of a little child.

When Peter gets himself into a bit of a scrape over Jesus' responsibility to pay temple tax (Matt 17:24-27), Jesus opens things up with a question, helps Peter to think through the principles and then offers him a pragmatic way out.

Picking up the pieces

One last set of observations on Jesus' skill as a mentor: Jesus does not just initiate, he also follows up. Perhaps the first time we notice this is, again, in the story where Jesus feeds the crowd. John tells us that Jesus specifically instructed his disciples to gather the leftovers so that nothing be wasted (John 6:12). Later that same evening, Jesus sends the disciples away while he disperses the crowd.

John notices and reports on Jesus' habit of following up the individual. He reports Jesus healing a man beside the pool of Bethesda (John 5:1-15). The chap takes some flak from the religious authorities for carrying his mat on the Sabbath so Jesus finds him later on to touch base. The same pattern emerges in John 9, where the blind man has an exhilarating struggle with the authorities before Jesus finds him and reveals more truth to him (John 9:35-39). Most poignantly, Jesus has a searching chat with Peter in John 21.

How many times have we done something dramatic, been involved in a clash, or started something off, and never gone back to make sure those affected are OK? After-sales care is one of the great differentiators in the market place. The garage that walks away from your problems will never sell you another car. In fact competition is often so intense that such players are likely to be out of business long before you get the chance to switch vendors. And yet our churches are full of people who have started out. They have started out as Christians but no-one has taken them on in the faith. They have started out as Sunday school teachers and no-one has looked in on their despondent muddle. They have had a fight with the vicar who is now unable to re-engage and do anything useful for them. Jesus does not have time for everything or everyone, but he makes time to finish things off – even if the conversation must be brief.

Pulling it all together

You may be worried that I have not factored in the impact of Pentecost on the success of the early church. Let me just say that, without the Holy Spirit, there would have been no early church. Pentecost changed the disciples – no doubt about it. But it was not a haphazard change. It wasn't a random flash. It was in line with the training that Jesus has been giving them. And to the same end.

My purpose here has been to explore the sort of training Jesus gave his disciples in terms we are familiar with. It is not to suggest that application of modern small group working on its own will make a church work as it might make a research or marketing group work. It won't, and I hope you have never believed it would.

But even a brief skim through Jesus' interaction with his disciples shows him to have been expert with tools and skills which we may regard as modern. Jesus was aware of group dynamics and made groups work. The gospel writers present us with a mentor who is active, who thinks ahead, and who keeps an eye on the individuals within the group. Jesus' approach may be more directive than that of many modern exponents of team work theory and this comes across very clearly in his teaching – which we consider in chapter 5.

Thinking it through

1. Why do you think Jesus decided not to write anything down? How might that decision have been related to the Holy Spirit's later work through the gospel writers and others?

2. In view of Jesus' practice of praying in public and of being seen engaging in prayer, by his disciples anyway, what do you make of his teaching that you should go to your room and pray in secret (Matt 6:5-15)?

3. Refer to Luke 9:18 and other relevant passages. How much privacy will a mentor lose?

4. Read the parable of the ten virgins (Matt 25:1-13). What are the main problems in interpreting it strictly as an allegory? Is the problem eased if we consider it more loosely as a tale of good habits and good preparation?

5. In the light of Jesus' teaching that earthly problems are easy but things to do with heaven and hell are hard, what agenda should mentors set: an agenda of signs and wonders – because these things are easy, or a lower profile agenda of prayer to target the really important things? How can a mentor discover the Holy Spirit's schedule?

6. How would you modify Jesus training methods in planning the following evangelistic campaigns:

   • A CU outreach at school?

   • An inner city event with an enthusiastic, recently converted, group of teenagers?

   • A relief and preaching operation to the Third World with working couples using 10 days of their annual leave?

7. What is the effect of seeing one's mentor under unbearable pressure? Where would you draw the line between great leadership in such circumstances and manipulation of one's followers? Can you find a non-biblical example for each side of the line?

8. What issues in a typical local church are worth offending people to get right?

9. List some aspects of Jesus' personal example that his disciples followed. Where do we see evidence that they understood and took them up?

3

Making the Most of Your Secular Training

Let's break off for a moment to explore some of the techniques that we consider routine at work but would not consider trying at church.

There is plenty of evidence in the New Testament outside the gospels that God was able to use people's training in very direct ways. The training Paul received under Gamaliel, though intended (and perhaps funded) for other ends, is marvellously used to tie together the most difficult Old Testament concepts with some of the most wonderful New Testament teaching. Luke's ability to describe situations, to interview people carefully, and his focus – as a physician – on fact is reflected in the literature he left behind. The buzz word is transferable skills: the things you learn in one career or job which can be applied to other tasks.

And, of course, as we survey the disciples, we find some evidence of transferable skills. Matthew, used to keeping records, leaves us a gospel. The fishermen, used to all-night sessions, danger and extreme exertion, discover that 'fishers of men' is more than mere word play.

We can make the point too strongly: as I say, I think stronger evidence exists elsewhere in the New Testament. But I guess there must be thousands, maybe tens of thousands of Christians like me in middle management, picking up training in listening, interviewing, people skills, time management, and all the rest, who never link it to their Christian service. I am not trying to exclude Christians not in management: soldiers, chippies, homemakers, plumbers or solicitors. I am just writing from where I stand, and hoping that others who stand somewhere else will be able to pick out the bits which apply to them.

As I look around I can also see dedicated Christians who have not benefited from such training, whose struggle in an indifferent, sometimes hostile, environment is only exacerbated by their lack of technique. How much easier their lives would be if only someone had taught them how to lay out an overhead projector presentation, or had spent some time with them on getting a lot done when you are already busy.

Don't get me wrong. At the end of the day, Jesus will build his church (Matt 16:18). If the gates of hell will not resist it, a slight shortage in the whizzo techniques department will not trouble the balance. It is just that, for many people, their training sits on the secular side of their lives, their Christian service lies on the other and it is highly unlikely that the two will ever become acquainted with one another.

Remember, Jesus calls people who are doing something else and sometimes it is because somebody else has already trained them to be effective. Jesus wants to use what we are. I am not saying that if you are a mechanic, you should seek your Christian service mending missionaries' jalopies, or run a car pool for full-time workers on furlough. I am not talking about that level of skill transfer. Nor am I suggesting that there are zippy shortcuts to spending time with God, meditating, or waiting for guidance.

But you may well have received thousands of pounds' worth of training, coaching and tuition during your career. Have you tried to draw the gold from the dross? Do you understand what is valuable about it? Have you tried to make it work in your house group? Your church? Do you think it might help your next venture into Christian service?

Secular training, Christian service

It is this synergy between Christian service and secular training that I believe merits more consideration in our culture. Personally, I have found some of the most difficult Christian issues have been presented to me through work. We often restrict our concept of integrity to not cheating on our expenses. What happens when your non-Christian boss accuses you of twisting the facts to win the argument? And yet a lack of integrity is at the heart of so many of our quarrels. Although we will pursue vendettas in our churches or on the mission field, sometimes for years, the problem is often a failure to examine the situation (or my impact on it) with a dispassionate integrity.

Isaiah has those unusual passages about Cyrus, the king who

released the Jews from their captivity in Babylon and allowed them to return home. He was not, as far as we know, a believer in God and yet Isaiah calls him God's anointed, and his shepherd, accomplishing God's will (Isa 44:27- 45:1). And for God's people in the modern world, God has cohorts of Cyruses, facing them up with their faults, challenging their concepts of holiness and generally rounding them up for heaven.

One of my most painful pieces of training was on a course where we were examining the things that motivated us and how well we lived up to our convictions. The team I was with knew something of the negative impact I could have on situations but I decided to trust to the process and put down the things I believed in. I put down honesty and then wondered what sort of qualities a Christian believes in. I had to start listing the fruit of the Spirit. You might have been wiser, and may be able to guess that the interaction got rather painful as we examined what I believed, and the results of some of my behaviour. You might like to try the exercise yourself some time. Put a poster on your wall (or in your window) which says, 'I believe in being loving, joyful, peaceful…'

But I learned something on the course that I had never heard from a pulpit – that the fruit of the Spirit is not something private. It is not about how you feel about yourself. It is about the environment you create around you every day at home, at work, at college or wherever. The secular advice I got was to lighten up and laugh a bit more. I have and I understand a bit more about living a unified life as a Christian in a working environment.

And yet our churches are full of Christians who believe themselves to be Spirit-filled, who are easily offended, people whom you have to work around in every situation, people who can turn anything into a chore simply by participating. I can't look down on them. Sometimes I am one of them. But I am learning to bear a different type of fruit.

And there are other good things in what we learn. There is some rediscovery of fundamental truths. It was Francis Schaeffer who reminded the church that all truth was God's truth. In our business-oriented world, a revived focus on people is refreshing and reflects something of the Bible's priorities. The ideas about teamwork and how groups of people achieve things are both ancient and modern. The way in which Jesus works with groups within groups (twelve out of the crowd and three out of the twelve) resonates strongly with many modern approaches. I am sure that you can look back over your training and pick up a spiritual dimension.

Making it count

So how do we identify what training is useful and apply it? In some ways the church has led the field with its development of home groups. The first-century church was well ahead of the modern pack in this respect. The small group work needs to be set in the right context – Jesus spoke to crowds, worked with small groups and reasoned with individuals. Used well, home groups offer an excellent opportunity to train disciples – finding out how people are really learning and providing a practical environment for implementing it all. Later on, when looking at Jesus with the disciples, we may gain some guidance for running our own small groups. All of this is well understood and there are many exponents of the cause more able than I am.

How could we take some of these ideas further? I would like to consider a few areas which are popular at the moment in commerce and industry and which may offer us some help in recognizing our own development and in developing others. Firstly, there is teamworking – and what we can do with it. Building on that, there is the question of gifting and group dynamics. Then I would like us to consider communication – in its most superficial and technical sense, namely getting the message across. Finally, there is time management – its importance to Jesus, to the early church and, I hope to us. Having raised your hopes, I ought to say that this is exploratory stuff, encouraging you to think it through, and not a formal approach to any of these topics.

Teamwork...

We tried a missionary activity recently modelled on small group working, the sort you might encounter at a management training event. We had a basic scenario in which teams of people were going to select a candidate couple and send them to some part of the world. The scenarios unfolded during the afternoon and the slots from our visiting missionary couple were ten minutes each. Although the event required lots of preparation, many people were able simply to turn up and start participating, discovering, learning and thinking. What is most important in a person's make up if they are going to survive in that part of the world? What emotional characteristics will they need? Will they be able to rely on the local church for spiritual support? Does the local church need support? Has the government suppressed the local church?

Apart from the fact that we had fun, I looked around and found people learning all kinds of things. Someone was reading up about Islam and Buddhism, others were compiling lists of characteristics of the ideal candidate (emotional stability came out uniformly high). A team that I had thought would struggle to assemble the material on its country, came up trumps and plastered the walls with coloured photographs of Christian work, people they knew there, and the typical day of a local. They even had time to write a poem as an epitaph for the local graveyard. Really worthwhile.

I wasn't sure how to pull it all together at the end of the day. I think it was my wife who suggested using T-shirts – one per team – on which to write the characteristics of your ideal missionary for the task and part of the world your team had been working on. I think there was also space for gifts and training.

The next day, we took some of it back to the main church. The walls were covered with the results of the previous day's efforts and we had the T-shirts. One member of each team modelled theirs on the platform, while someone explained why the team had written the things they had on the T-shirt. For us it was experimental and had shortcomings – but it might be worth developing and building on. I had learned how to run events like that for work. The key, I had been taught, was to write down your aims, what you want to get out of the day – and then your objectives, the specific things your teams will produce (such as a list of characteristics, a description of a typical day, a T-shirt full of ideas). This was a chance to try it at church and, for the most part, it was a great day. And it is good stewardship – the characteristics washed out and I still wear the T-shirts!

A couple at our church have had a burden for a group of local evangelists with whom we are associated (along with other churches in the county), but whom we only really know as speakers. They planned a family day, gave it a wacky title, and invited families from our church and another church across town to come for an afternoon of games, making things, interviews and an early evening question and answer session with the four evangelists and their spouses. It was a great success. It was fun, informative and left us all feeling that we knew these people and understood their ministry better.

As a leadership team we had felt for some time the need to get away and develop some focus for the future. Someone found a hotel prepared to give us breakfast in a private room, coffee mid-morning, and leave us alone until midday. To kick things off, we ended up playing a game with 'post-its' where we each chose three things we wanted to keep and three things we would like to change. We went around picking up the common themes and sticking them together in short chains.

The agenda had been set to have a lot of prayer (in manageable slots), devotional times, discursive times, and times for sharing how we were with our families. The game at the start surprised me because, although we were all very different and often approached things very differently during our monthly get-togethers, there was a lot of consensus about what we wanted more and less of. It helped us to find some common themes to pray over and enabled us quickly to identify the one 'hot' topic we had time to plan around for the next few months.

These are just three examples of small group working being made to work in a church context. They are not particularly unusual, but they did work. They helped those involved to get more from the exercise and to buy into what was happening. It might be too mechanistic for some. I can only suggest that you build in more time for prayer and devotion. But I think it is worth experimenting with.

Some of the theory about what makes a team work (and most of us have had a brief skirmish with Belbin), resonates with the scriptural truth about gifting, about eyes and ears, feet and arms (1 Cor 12:12-31), and also what are sometimes referred to as motivational gifts (Rom 12:4-8). I hope it does not detract from the supernatural dimension implicit in gifting to see that some of the same principles are buried deep in humanity. The personality clashes between the creative type and the monitor-evaluator type also surface in church – although sometimes the theological context prevents us from seeing what is really happening. We tend to identify a conflict of principle before we seek a solution in a clash of personality, particularly in the gifting enjoyed by those involved. I have a hunch that some of the charismatic-non charismatic problems in local churches could be greatly eased if the gifts of each side were recognised and explored.

But that is just a hunch. I am neither a psychologist nor a theologian. I am just trying to bring together issues at the level at which they have reached me – in training and in life. I understand that those who have made a point of assembling their leadership teams with motivational gifting in mind report on how much better things go.

Style with content

There is also a lot of emphasis these days on communication: how you gain people's attention; how to make a presentation; how to lay out your overhead projector transparencies, or acetates ('if you couldn't fit it on a T-shirt, don't put it on an acetate'); how to keep the talk short; how to gauge whether people are listening to you.

These techniques will not turn a poorly thought out talk into anything other than a well presented, but useless talk. If I were forced on the point, I would have to say that content, rather than communication style is the greater shortcoming of our era. However, as part of proper preparation, these techniques can drive a good message home, help a congregation to understand what is important to you in the talk and make it stick in the mind. The verve and flair which drives a good sales pitch makes for punchy gospel epilogues. Evangelists such as Billy Graham and D L Moody were great salesmen before they were great preachers. I have also found the converse to be true: that the conviction and the degree of fluency which comes from talks at church will often help in tackling topics at work.

So how do we bring style and content together? One caricature of our churches might be that those who are long on style are short on content – and vice versa. There are probably dozens of ways of addressing the issue of style with content. I had a fun time recently with a bunch of the lads at church. One of them had said he would like to do a service and so, having thought about it, the leadership offered them the chance to do a series. More of them turned up to the first planning meeting than I had expected.

I had chosen a rather ambitious theme – five weeks of Ezra and Nehemiah with four slots to be filled by the team (a visiting speaker having been booked already for the fifth slot). As the team began to put the facts together with the problems, together with scenarios not too different from modern situations, the lights went on in their eyes and you could see that they were connecting with the text. Over the weeks they learned and I learned. I learned why the amount of content I tend to throw into a talk can leave an audience baffled. They wanted to focus on one or two points and that was all. And it worked. People left with one point in their mind from each week.

The aim of the experiment for me was to see how we could build content together, exploiting the undeniable style of the team. One evening the ideas were really fizzing. We wanted to convey the message that Ezra, Nehemiah and Zerubbabel, with their different gifts, backgrounds, jobs, training and places in society, were all chosen by God and that it was the combination of their ministries that pulled the Jewish people through a very tough time. They came up with a game show format, and we flirted with a rather famous scenario (without wishing to advertise a particular show) in which one person chooses someone from a group of three by asking questions. It took some thinking to keep it on the right side of the tracks as far as reverence was concerned and to make the particular point we wanted to make about all three being chosen. But we got there. The product was funny, the message identifiable, we learned and were able to pass something on. And they presented everything on their own.

Both the style of the finished product (short episodes of prayer, talk, sketch or worship filling out the time traditionally allocated to the speaker) and the way in which we got there involved small group working. I am not offering a blueprint. Merely saying that we found a way fairly quickly, so the evidence is that you could do the same with a little planning and a willingness to make mistakes.

And we made mistakes – not everything we tried came off. For me, however, the great payoff was that the last in the series was (in my opinion) a really well presented Sunday Morning. Others had been very good – but the last had that touch of polish. Secondly, the group that finished the course, so to speak, was quite different from the one that started. The starters were unsure about themselves and the text. The same people at the finish knew what they were about. It was quite funny because halfway through, someone else joined the team. He would ask very sensible questions – and the others would jump on him as though the answers were obvious. Until that happened, I don't believe any of us had realized how far the group had developed in its understanding. Incidentally, the newcomer did really well when his turn came to present.

Squeezing it in

Have you ever noticed how the best way to get something done at church is to ask someone who is already busy? The people who are stretched are stretchable. Time management techniques (formally taken in or informally developed) are working for them and enable them to do more. I have a friend who has cut his NIV paperback Bible into three sections, so that he can always have one of them in his inside jacket pocket with him on the train. Others who commute by car use the Bible on tapes. Thoughtful Christians have always been into time management: when my Dad was at Bible school in the '50s there was a chap at his church who had taught himself Greek on the tube to work.

Today there is a vast array of useful tips in a formal framework calling itself time management. Some of it will prove useless to you, but some of it may help. It is just another example of the world around realising that it has to make the most of every opportunity (Eph 5:16). Jesus encouraged his disciples: 'As long as it is day, we must do the work of him who sent me. Night is coming, when no-one can work' (John 9:4).

Jesus' complete mastery of his time is one of the magnificent features of his life. There is time for the crowds and in a crowded diary there is time for individuals. Jesus knows how to power nap in a fishing boat caught in a storm (Mark 4:35-41), knows how to break away from a successful mission in order to fit in other missions (Mark 1:35-39), and is amazingly curt with time wasters (Luke 9:57-62). For me, the story of the Syro-Phoenician woman (Mark 7:24-30) only makes sense if Jesus has a schedule, a set of priorities which involves leaving some things undone in order to achieve the tasks he has been set by the Father. I believe that it is only this woman's amazing faith that blasts her up the priority list and elicits the response she so badly needs. Because faith comes top of the list with Jesus.

Thinking it over

I hope the last few pages have persuaded you that you need not know a great deal about a technique to think about how it might apply to your Christian service or leadership. Clearly, there are areas to be approached with caution. Some categories of counselling and even shepherding might fit in there. But between doing nothing and doing something dangerous lies a vast swathe of methods, ideas and techniques that have something to offer. You will have some experience in applying them to get your job done – how about thinking how they help with the task in hand at church?

One of the things I love about watching the kids is to see how they improvise. Earlier on this afternoon, my toddler wanted a drink that was just out of reach. It wasn't his drink, but his brother was miles away – so who cares? Anyway, he can't reach the drink directly, but he can swish an empty laundry bag lying just behind it. And whoosh, the drink (mercifully complete with non-spill nozzle) is lying on the floor beside him. Improvisation. Success. Bibulous contentment.

And kids will do that every time. They get hold of words and make them work for them. They climb up on stools, packing cases, even on each other to get their hands on the unreachable. They turn sticks and spoons into tools and force out the result they want. They do not wait until they understand it all before they attempt anything. They pick up the mouse and start clicking years before they will understand the magnetics behind a disk drive or the logic behind an operating system.

Of course Little Man scattered some papers lying next to the drink. Sometimes God helps us to realise that papers will get scattered and gives us the wisdom to try another approach. Sometimes God gives us the patience to pick up the papers, or the pieces, or whatever. But let's try. Our world has laid so much emphasis on training at the expense of genuine education that we are losing the confidence to think a thing through, and to apply what used to be called sanctified common sense. I am not advocating wild abandon in pursuit of every new whim. Those who know me best would complain that I am vocally in favour of sitting down and thinking things through. But having thought about it let's be experimental. Let's hang onto the good things and let the failures fade quickly into insignificance.

You probably have questions about the validity of the training you get. Maybe that is why it helps to keep it in a separate compartment from anything Christian. Modern ideas are based around persuading people rather than instructing or directing them. The underlying assumptions are that people are basically good and mean well, while a Christian perspective presents humanity as fatally flawed, awash with all kinds of primal instincts, urges and suspect motivation. The modern manager will often nurture and ultimately exploit personal ambition or ambition in others, while scripture identifies human selfishness as lying near the very heart of our problem – early and ubiquitous evidence of our fundamental rebellion against God.

I have not invested enough thought and lack the background to do justice to the issue. I can only raise it and encourage other Christians to address it. However, the most important thing is for you to examine the questions in your situation. The very process of bringing what we learn to God, in prayer, in our devotions, perhaps as a group activity in discussion, helps us to meet our responsibility of taking our faith seriously.

I think Paul is talking about something similar, albeit with more martial an imagery, when he says: 'For though we live in the world, we do not wage war as the world does. The weapons we fight with are not the weapons of the world. On the contrary, they have divine power to demolish strongholds. We demolish arguments and every pretension that sets itself up against the knowledge of God, and we take captive every thought to make it obedient to Christ' (2 Cor 10:3-5).

Clearly, a blind acceptance of modern training techniques will lead us to wage war as the world does. However, each time we bring our learning to the standard of God's word, we leave with a better understanding both of scripture and of the situation we brought along. Each time we illuminate a concept with the truth of scripture, we see its fault lines clearly. While some of our training may support our service, this exercise of taking 'captive every thought' will help us to detect the undercurrents in the modern scene and, where necessary, to swim against the tide.

Our churches are full of people with insight, training and transferable skills which somebody else has paid for and which can be highly effective as part of a life dedicated to serving Jesus. The training is not magical, but it may be part of what you are now – and an important part of you at that. Some of the thinking behind the methods may be flawed, and as a Christian you need to understand the flaws and avoid the associated pit-falls. Even so, I believe there is a sense in which, 'to the pure all things are pure' (Tit 1:15). As such, God can use them and you. Don't take your secular training for granted, ignore it, or relegate it to a part of your life which has nothing to do with Jesus.

Thinking it through

1. In the light of this chapter, consider Nehemiah's gifts and transferable skills. How do you think these had made him successful at the palace? How did they make him effective in rebuilding the walls of Jerusalem?

2. Is there any evidence that Jesus planned his time? If so, in what ways might Jesus' time planning be like ours and in what ways might it be radically different? If not, are there any other models that we might use to explain the effectiveness of his interactions?

3. Judging from the way in which Jesus lived his life, what would you say were his top three or four priorities? List three or four things that matter to you that would not have mattered to Jesus at all.

4. 'What is this? A new teaching...!' (Mark 1:27). Make a list of all the communication techniques that Jesus used. To what extent were they new and different?

5. To what extent has the church failed to be people-centred? How has this affected its internal function and its mission to the world around? What are the dangers of being too people-centred?

6. In terms of the way you spend the time in your home group, what are the top three priorities? From the things Jesus did with small groups, what would you say were his priorities? How good is the overlap?

7. What are the differences between self-respect, self-interest and selfishness?

8. Read John 4. Do you think Jesus was prepared for his encounter with the Samaritan woman, and if so, how and when do you think he had prepared?

4

How Do You Get the Right Question?

Almost any course you attend on appraisals, interviewing, conflict resolution or the like will stress the importance of questions. We have to learn to stop telling and start asking. And then we have to learn how to ask – questions that open up a situation, questions that clarify, questions that verify, questions that set people at their ease, questions that search their souls, questions that help us to understand what is really going on.

In this context, questioning can become a routine, perhaps even a superficial business. But questions still lie at the heart of our whole thinking process. While there are plenty of trivial, tangential and time-wasting questions, the right question will blast a puzzle wide open. Good questions are worth carrying around in the back pocket of your mind to explore and examine from time to time. Great questions will last you the rest of your life.

Children are great at questions. They have a thirst for understanding that drives a withering, incessant stream of questions. It is the most draining and stimulating thing about them. And so often, they knock you off your balance. I remember talking to one of my brothers about heaven when he was very young. 'Can I ride my bike there?' His ideas of heaven have changed since then and the new bike is now only a memory, but the question is still good, for: 'Where your treasure is, there your heart will be also' (Luke 12:34). And the question throws a searching beam on my own soul.

Jesus' life was full of questions. Questions people asked him, questions he asked them, rhetorical questions, probing questions, questions to flush people out of the shadows, questions to haunt them forever. Then there were the questions people asked about Jesus: questions he manages to intercept – or ignore. And Jesus' mastery of the question still stuns.

The trick question

I suppose it is the trick question that first opens our awareness of Jesus' skill in this arena. Even though I have read the story many times, the 'taxes to Caesar' question (Mark 12:13-17) still sparkles and awes. Mark reports, 'And they were amazed at him' (12:17). Almost two millennia on, I still am. Perhaps more than our predecessors, we know the damage that can be inflicted by a well prepared question. I don't know which radio or television station supports your favourite interviewer but we have a high regard for these questioners and nothing but admiration for the handful of public figures who enter the fray and emerge unscathed.

And here is Jesus up against the brightest minds of his generation, who have crafted their question with care. In a busy day, Jesus is ambushed by scholars with the time to get their act together: 'Is it right to pay taxes to Caesar or not?' For me, Jesus' brilliance lies in finding the right question before he delivers the right answer. 'Whose portrait is this? And whose inscription?' Does Jesus' question buy him time? Does it show objectivity, a desire to focus on the facts behind the subterfuge? Whatever the process, Jesus uses it to demolish the high moral ground which they think they occupy, discovering their pockets ajingle with Caesar's currency. Then he drags a 'Caesar' from their own mouths. He wants them involved in the answer. The fun thing about Jesus' question is that they are undone before they realise it. Jesus' final response is just the coup de grace. I love the story every time I read it, and the more I understand about questions, the more awed I am.

But in the middle of all the hostile questions, Jesus is listening. He hears the heartache, the worry, even some unexpected integrity. Later in the same chapter, at the end of a lengthy and probing question and answer session, Jesus picks up a serious note of sincerity and tells the lawyer, 'You are not far from the kingdom of God' (Mark 12:34).

Questions people asked about Jesus

So how will we tackle the topic of questions and Jesus? Well let's begin with the questions people asked about Jesus. How can Jesus be master of those questions? Well, whatever the reasons behind them we have to say that people asked a lot of questions about Jesus. Jesus led a life that drew questions out of people. As a model leader and leadership trainer, Jesus saves himself a lot of aggro by managing to get people to ask useful questions. People who have asked a question entirely off their own bat are usually more open to an answer. Sometimes Jesus picks up on these questions. Sometimes they just linger. Sometimes they waft down the centuries to us.

In our age and culture we spend a lot of time trying to attract people's attention. Perhaps we would be more effective if we concentrated instead on the right lifestyle, and allowed that to attract the questions. Certainly that seems to have been Jesus' approach.

Mark seems to be particularly interested in questions and his gospel provides a helpful place to start examining the questions in Jesus' life. A helpful exercise is to skim through the first few chapters of Mark's gospel listing the questions people asked about Jesus. Here is a sample:

- 'What is this? A new teaching – and with what authority!' (1:27)
- 'Why does this fellow talk like that? …Who can forgive sins but God alone?' (2:7)
- 'Why does he eat with tax collectors and "sinners"?' (2:16)
- 'Who is this? Even the wind and the waves obey him!' (4:41)
- 'Isn't this the carpenter? Isn't this Mary's son…?' (6:3; see also 6:2)

Now, why had people asked the question? What was it that Jesus had just said or done which they had not expected? Was it the style? The theology? The sheer unthinkability of what they had just witnessed? To what extent are you and I called to lead a life that raises those sorts of questions in people's minds? What sort of questions should people be asking about a Christian who lives where you live and does what you do?

Notice that Jesus makes it his business to know what people are asking about him. Sometimes Jesus knows supernaturally (e.g. Mark 2:8), at other times it is reasonable to assume he overhears (e.g. Mark 2:17). Mark 8:27 will at least bear the interpretation that Jesus keeps his finger on the pulse of public opinion by asking his disciples what the word is on the street, though the thrust of that passage clearly lies elsewhere.

So what is there here for us? Do we know the questions people are asking about us? Are they the sort of questions which we
can make use of? Let's be honest, many of the questions people
ask about us will provide us with an agenda for improvement
rather than an opportunity for witness. Most questions about us
go like this: 'How can he/she do... and still be a Christian?'
Don't be disappointed! In my experience, a lot of management
training lies in discovering that you have plenty of scope for
improvement. Take up the challenge, consider the questions
and, if necessary, ask God to help you change your lifestyle.

But people may well ask better questions about you. They
may admire you for things you would rather they did not. Perhaps your faith has enabled you to remain cheerful despite having a hostile partner. Perhaps they wonder how you cope with
bereavement, or handle physical setbacks in life. Perhaps they
are amazed at your attitude to personal poverty. You might
much rather they admired you for your wit or wisdom, for
being the life and soul of the party, or for your earning power.
Surely the point is that if we are to influence others, we must
lead a life which stimulates the right sort of questions and use
those questions to the glory of God rather than for personal
gratification. It is a lesson I am learning and I will try to give you
an illustration once I have mastered the method.

Questions people asked Jesus

What about the questions people asked Jesus? Have you ever
seen someone making a mess of things and not been sure how
to help? You know that if you weigh in with your view it may
be resented and will almost certainly have little impact. But
what if they come asking you? That is a different ball game.
Firstly, you find out if your initial evaluation was right before
you make any suggestions. Then you get a chance to tune your
response to better meet the need. Finally, it is more likely that
your advice will have an impact – particularly if you can find a
simple, practical, short-term suggestion that your questioner
can try out in order to build some confidence in your advice.

So what sort of a person do people want to take their questions to? Do they always get it right? Well, whom do I go to for
help? I had something the other night that was worrying me
and I wanted some people to pray about it for me. Looking

back, I guess there were two things that shaped my choice. I went for people whom I thought competent (in this case, people who prayed and believed in praying things through) and people who were available – someone I might have asked was out.

I guess much the same applies to the people who came to Jesus. Perhaps he refuses to dialogue with some people in order to be available for others more likely to respond. And so Jesus declines the invitation to mediate between brothers over the inheritance (Luke 12:13,14) although he takes the opportunity to turn the question latent in the request from equity to eternity. The three people who seem to want so much to follow Jesus are quickly put off (Luke 9:57-62) and Jesus does not pursue the rich young man once it is clear where his heart lies (Mark 10:17-22).

While we could spend a lot of time exploring the sort of life Jesus led and trying to emulate it, it will probably help us here to focus instead on how Jesus dealt with the questions once they came. Rather than wishing that more people came asking for our advice, we might prepare ourselves to offer better support to the next person who comes along. After all, somebody, sometime has come to each of us with a question. How often have we been caught off-guard, muttered something innocuous or inane, and then wondered vaguely why people do not seek us out more often?

The rich young man whom we have just encountered is a good example of someone coming to Jesus. Jesus does not have the time to enrol people in preparatory classes (although, in a sense, God had been running an introductory session on a grand scale since Moses and the Law). But, by and large, the encounter is it. First time round is all there is time for.

So what matters to Jesus? What is he after in those first few moments? Well our rich young man's body language is excellent – he kneels to ask his question. He has a sense of need and his question is succinct (Mark 10:17): 'What must I do to inherit eternal life?' Jesus has a surprising question in return, 'Why do you call me good? No-one is good – except God alone. You know the commandments…'

I have to confess that I am stumped by Jesus' responding question. Was there a long pause before Jesus begins to reel off the commandments? Or does Jesus throw in the question and move on, sure that it will be many years before young Rich really understands the significance of opening up with, 'Good teacher'? Was there something too gushing in his approach, which had already alerted Jesus to a desire to be seen to be asking a good question rather than listening to a good answer? We do not know. I do not understand the cultural cross-ply underlying the encounter.

But Jesus sets about testing his resolve to find an answer. And young Rich duly obliges. He will not drop it. The most alarming thing about encounters with Jesus is the speed with which he gets to the heart of the problem, rather than massaging the symptoms. Young Rich is suddenly faced with the fact that he can only get what he really wants by letting go of what he really loves. And this encounter goes no further.

Jesus' early questions seem to probe around the motivation issue. Mark 10 is a good chapter for this. James and John want special favours. 'What do you want me to do for you?' is Jesus' question to them as it is to Bartimaeus whose yelling above the crowd finally grants him the audience he wants so much (Mark 10:36,37). Perhaps the sons of Zebedee rather wished they had not been quite so grandiose or explicit with their request (10:41ff). But Jesus gets it all into the open. He is able to use their slip to teach more important lessons to the Twelve. And because they have stated it in their own words they cannot explain away their ambition afterwards. They know what they were really after – and so do the rest of the disciples.

But why get Bartimaeus to state what he wants? I guess it removes any ambiguity. He is not after wealth, nor do the pressures of eternity seem to drive his sense of need. He wants to see. And when he responds, everything is clear – to everyone. Long before opening questions became trendy, we see Jesus using them as a tool, enabling people to state what they really want, sometimes forcing people to face up to the full impact of their aspirations.

Of course lots of people came to Jesus simply because they had an obvious need: they were ill, they had friends who were ill, their friends or members of their families suffered demonic possession, they were hungry. And because Jesus met their need, they came back. Jesus says as much in John 6:26: 'I tell you the truth, you are looking for me, not because you saw miraculous signs but because you ate the loaves and had your fill.'

In passing, we have here another clue about why people come back for more – because they get what they need first time around. I am not sure that we always want the joy that comes from that type of person returning for more. Jesus' advice is stunningly simple: 'Give to the one who asks you, and do not turn away from the one who wants to borrow from you' (Matt 5:42). And Jesus lives by his own advice – once the situation is clear, he does not interrogate them about the desirability of dependence or explore routes towards rehabilitation. He gives them what they ask for. Jesus knows when to cut the questions and act.

Another digression: even little things impact on the world around us. I am not just talking about how you react to a beggar in the tube. How about the leaving card going around the office? A sponsorship form from a neighbour? When someone is selling lottery tickets for the school fete? The secretaries in the office told me that they knew who would sign a leaving card but contribute nothing. I hope those non-contributors were not Christian leaders in training. You just do not know who is watching the most innocent request. Or how one can build a positive reputation simply by giving freely to what is going around.

Before leaving this, we need to see that, while Jesus is very switched on to questions, he does not approach people as a modern therapist. He does not often behave as though he believes the answer lies deep inside the individual. There will be times when he will tease out the answer that he knows they have inside. The story of the Samaritan woman in John 4 is perhaps an example of Jesus at his most patient and intriguing, determined not to apply answers until his conversationalist is in the right frame of mind. However, even then, Jesus has to reveal new things to her. There is a dimension of revelation and knowledge that underpins Jesus' approach to questions and we will have to come back to this later.

Discussion and debate

So what about the other sorts of questions? Apart from the trick questions, there was plenty of hard argument, the verbal slog as people began to realise what Jesus was really saying, and went in blazing. 'Why are they doing what is unlawful on the Sabbath?' (Mark 2:24). 'Why don't your disciples live according to the tradition of the elders…?' (Mark 7:5). 'Is it lawful for a man to divorce his wife?' (Mark 10:2).

Jesus' approach, as we have come to expect, is usually to ask a question that examines the source of their authority – for Jesus and for them that meant the Old Testament scriptures. 'Have you never read what David did?' (Mark 2:25). 'What did Moses command you?' (Mark 10:3). In Mark 7, however, Jesus goes straight for the jugular, blasting away at them for putting their own ideas above the authority of scripture. But often there is that second, penetrating question. How many theological questions do we field with an enquiry about the most relevant passages of scripture? How many times do we have the background or the courage to go back to first principles and to take our questioner with us?

We face a problem in our day and age that Jesus did not have. We have already noted the fact that God had spent a great deal of time preparing a people that knew scripture. For first-century Jews, it was a given that God's word contained the answers to life and everything else. Paul understands the importance of revelation and scripture when he writes to the Jewish contingent in Rome (Rom 2:17,18): 'Now you, if you call yourself a Jew; if you rely on the law and brag about your relationship to God; if you know his will and approve of what is superior because you are instructed by the law...'

Despite the fact that our generation has problems here, we cannot underestimate the importance of going back to scriptural basics in debate. Even when people used the Old Testament to construct elaborate scenarios to prove their case, Jesus goes back further to re-examine the basics. Remember the Sadducees, with their question about seven brothers who managed to die, childless and in sequence? Under the Mosaic law, the eldest brother's widow partnered each brother in turn until, in a sadly amusing finale, 'last of all, the woman died too' (Mark 12:22). Jesus manages to get back to a time before Moses and the Law, to Moses and the burning bush (Exodus 3:6), asserting that Abraham, Isaac and Jacob were alive and that God was their God even then.

'You are badly mistaken!' (Mark 12:27) is Jesus' verdict on their approach. Why? Because they did not understand their scriptures nor God's power (Mark 12:24). What would be his verdict on so much modern analysis?

How do we go back to basics today?

Our first problem is that many Christians do not have the faith in scriptural solutions to make it their first port of call in a crisis. Secondly, most Christians' grasp of what the Bible actually says is so tenuous that anyone who takes this approach is seen as a threat – a sort of super-administrator whose paralysing power comes from knowing the rules better than anyone else. The framework for the sort of dialectic in which Jesus engaged has been seriously eroded.

All is not lost! Jesus manages a very fruitful conversation with the Samaritan woman in John 4 despite the lack of a common moral framework. And Jesus starts it with a question! Here Jesus is able to bridge the gap, partly on the basis of her honesty about her personal need. With centurions, Jesus connects over the exercise of authority (Luke 7:1-10) or the sheer quality of his life and death (Luke 23:47). Any evangelist will list a host of ways in which this type of bridge can be built. I'm not an evangelist and recommend that you go along and hear one for yourself. God has blessed churches of all flavours with some wonderfully gifted evangelists who are well worth hearing. Their talks are worth dissecting so that we can make our own witness more effective.

In the middle of writing this chapter I had a chance to try out my own advice. We had had a delegation of young people visit the leadership to discuss a number of issues, including our communion service. Eventually, as a result, my wife and I managed to fit in an evening of pizza and discussion. Using a couple of games, we assembled a list of what people liked and disliked about the current situation – surprisingly close in many aspects to the leadership's own joys and concerns.

To get some input from the Bible, we split into two groups to produce a couple of quick posters, one about the early church's communion and the other examining how we should be the same and where and why we might differ. Armed with a list of potentially relevant passages and a pile of Bibles, the two teams made swift progress. For me, the most encouraging part was the way in which, during the subsequent presentation and discussion of their findings, the teams tracked back to what they had looked up. The final game which extracted a list of things that they could do to ameliorate the unpleasant and accentuate the enjoyable, showed that they had taken in a number of the messages latent in the text. I know people are unlikely to eat your pizza and then carp about your approach, but one of them did comment on how nice it had been to have a structured discussion on the topic.

My guess is that there is scope for this approach in addressing all kinds of questions. Sometimes we are much more interested in airing our views or even venting our spleens than we are in knuckling down to some preparation for a fruitful discussion. And it does take the effort. You probably won't find a resource book yet on Menus for Money Management, Fondues on the Family, or Churches and Chip butties. They will come, I am sure, but you will have to do your own spadework for now. Your young people will actually do extremely well, here. The older folk may well have a background Bible knowledge that helps them overcome the barrier of this whole new approach to discussion. How your families and the middle-aged will fare, I have no idea. Let me know.

As well as this, however, we do need restoration experts to repair the damaged foundations. We need Christian thinkers to see the issues coming before the world around tackles them. The church could have had a position on ecology before the Greens got there. Now that the debate is polarised, our main options lie in remaining with the regressives or trying to find a spiritual hue for our own shade of green.

There is a growing range of issues where Christian leaders have lacked the confidence in, or the knowledge of, scripture to carve out a truly scriptural approach which trusts God to have gotten it right. Surely there is a more thoroughly Christian approach to counselling, the place and role of education or the elderly, to sex, gender or the family than the approaches we tend to take, reliant as they are on analysis provided by the world around us – or a direct reaction against it.

This is not a call for old-fashioned values but for Christian thinkers to free themselves of modern dogmas and to see what scripture has to say to us today. That has always been the job of Christian thinkers and teachers. One reason we take such a dim view of basic values in retrospect is that we only see them long after they have atrophied beyond meaningful practice.

For instance, is Sunday school simply perpetuated by loyal Christian parents, or non-Christian parents looking forward to a relaxing spell at home? We do not see the innovation Robert

Raikes introduced in its context of the underprivileged, or appreciate its impact as genuinely pious teachers saw God at work in young lives. If we have any picture of him, it is likely to be of a statue along the Embankment. From our perspective, we cannot easily appreciate how, along with other movements, it transformed the face of our nation. With society vastly changed in terms of education, leisure, opportunities, the working environment and all the rest, the concept of Sunday school may well be ripe for reconsideration. I have heard of at least one thriving church that ditched Sunday school in favour of a weeknight event.

I am not trying to make the point on Sunday schools one way or another here – merely to indicate that many of the things we regard as old-fashioned principles may be neither old-fashioned nor principles. It is just that we see the worst about them because our perspective prevents us from seeing them in anything like their prime. Secondly, they did represent an appropriate embodiment of principle for their era. We may have to find a new embodiment of those same principles to be faithful witnesses in our own generation.

As a final example, we are unlikely to discover that a simple re-affirmation of family values will magically transform the tangles in which so much of our society (and particularly, therefore, our new intake of Christians) are trapped. Going back to basics, I do not see that the Apostles would have required a bigamist to ditch one wife if he had two on conversion. Rather, I see that, by requiring monogamy of church leaders and teaching the practice to new converts, they ushered in a profound cultural change. I know of at least one missionary in France who has gone back and re-examined cohabitation because of a number of cohabitees coming to church having one partner who has met Jesus in a transforming way.

Two thousand years on, the social lining is unravelling. We have to go back to basics to discover how to re-introduce cultural change, based again on scripture, on leadership prepared to stand up to the mark and on the willingness of millions of insignificant Christians to live by it.

Open answers

This is not a manual on questioning techniques for leaders. It is a little shout to say, Hey! Before all the manuals on questions, Jesus was there. He was a profoundly questioning person and he raised questions in other people's minds. You will gather that I have pretty well reached my limit. Someone else can do the systematic stuff and pull it all together in a unified way. Just read the gospels, jump up and down when you find a question and use that as a launch pad for your own devotions.

However, we cannot leave this topic without looking at the times when Jesus does not ask questions. If Mark is the man for the questions, John is unquestionably the expert on one-to-one encounters.

Here the questions seem to come the other way. Nicodemus (John 3) and, after the ice-breaking question, the Samaritan woman (John 4) both sustain the conversation with their questions or requests. My favourite encounter is with the blind man in John 9, but it is not until most of the action is over (and robust, encouraging stuff it is, too) that Jesus pops the really deep question, 'Do you believe in the Son of Man?' (John 9:35b).

We see, then, that Jesus also has an amazing technique with what we might call open answers. If open questions give rise to further discussion, open answers usher in yet more questions. Go through the passages in John and look at the way in which Jesus talks about interesting things in such a wonderfully mysterious way that people cannot help but ask questions. Jesus has identified what is of interest to his conversational partner early on and is willing to talk about that. The rest defies analysis as far as I am concerned – but there is something attractive about Jesus' replies. You sometimes catch the flavour of it today. There are people whom you just want to listen to, people who can open up a topic in such fascinating style that you do not want the conversation to conclude.

Can we learn from that? Maybe. We can certainly identify the people who have the gift and find them special roles in our outreach, churches, or events. We can also focus more on what interests people than on what interests us in a conversation. Other than that, all I can do, probably all I am able to do, with any of this is to point out the interesting scenery we are rambling through and hope some of it means something to you.

Thinking it through

1. 'Jesus replied, "I will ask you one question."' Read Mark 11:27-33. Is this question a defensive parry or a strategic thrust? What issues were at stake? How has Jesus answered his critics? What about the onlookers?

2. 'Is it not written...?' Read Mark 11:15-18. Why do you think Jesus chose this particular quotation? What does the wider passage in Isaiah 56 tell us about Jesus' purpose? What do you think the full impact would have been on the chief priests and teachers of the law who would have recognised the quotation instantly?

3. Read Matthew 11:7-19. How does Jesus use questions in teaching the crowd? What central message has he succeeded in making memorable?

4. Read John 21:15-19. How does Jesus use a rather narrow question to probe the recesses of Peter's soul? What does Jesus achieve with this approach? What did Peter learn from it? What do we learn?

5. 'Do you still not see or understand?' Read Mark 8:14-21. How do you think Jesus felt? If humanity was surprised by Jesus, what aspects of humanity seem to have surprised or frustrated Jesus?

6. 'What were you arguing about on the road?' Read Mark 9:33-37. Why did Jesus not ask this question at the time? What sort of questions are best left until later?

7. What do you think really mattered to Nicodemus? What sort of things attracted his interest? What topics would have turned him off?

5

Leading from the Front

How you are taught probably has a lot to do with what you have to learn. I remember attending an event for science and technology teachers in the county. My company wanted someone to talk about science in industry and I seized the chance – events like that always interest me and there was an after-dinner speaker whom I wanted to hear.

Whenever I come across teachers I am impressed by the way they understand the mechanism of teaching. On this occasion, I sat in on a seminar where a group was introduced to a new piece of equipment based around fibre optics. For most of them, this was new territory but they were already working out how they would use this kit to teach. Over lunch we got talking about learning by rote and through discovery. Apparently discovery learning is highly effective but it takes ages if that is the only approach.

And Jesus doesn't have ages. Nor do doctors who have to assimilate a massive learning load, develop observational and experimental techniques and take on behavioural skills within a few years. I cannot judge the pedagogic balance of modern medical training but it is not hard to see why these pressures have led to the ward round, that whirl of drama, theory, practice, and occasional humiliation, which the experienced deem essential and the students dread.

And it is hard to read the gospels without at least a whiff of the ward round. In a very public society, Jesus holds everything up to public scrutiny. Personal faith is publicly commended, private flaws inexorably condemned. Any incident is fair game, providing a basis for discussion or a launching pad for a parable.

Stop the world!

Let's flick through Matthew, starting at chapter 8 (we can come back to Jesus' formal teaching later) and pick up with the centurion at Capernaum (Matt 8:5-13). The story is so full of incident, pace and colour and so bursting with questions, that it is easy to get distracted. How could Jesus be astonished? In a world that generally surprised him with its inability to grasp the obvious, what was it that caught him unawares about this chap? And why, having been caught on the hop, does Jesus turn to the crowd? Even before granting the chap's request!

Jesus has found something he really values. He wants others to understand its value, and so he stops and draws attention to it. The servant will be healed, the centurion will get on with his life, the crowds will continue to press with their needs and will drift past once those needs are met, but this moment is worth stopping the world for. Jesus cannot be too extravagant in his analysis. He draws in Abraham, Isaac and Jacob. He pictures crowds of foreigners, rather like this centurion, sitting down to eat with the patriarchs while their descendants are chucked out. It is hard to imagine a greater compliment for the centurion or a more severe reprimand for his audience.

So why does he risk antagonising the good folk of Capernaum? Why inflame every raw, nationalistic nerve? Why risk being misunderstood in such delicate territory? Well, Jesus has seen a spot of faith, and faith is like gold dust. You can't have too much of it, but even a little is incredibly valuable in Jesus' economy. Heaven ticks on faith.

And this is all about values. As part of his values-changing mission, we find Jesus picking up on things that people think insignificant – because they don't really matter in this world.

Notice also that it takes a lot of focus to see the opportunity to praise someone with the right values. As a manager, I always found it easier to spot the deficiencies and then try to sort them out. The more pressurized you are, the harder it is to disengage from critical mode and to focus on the good things that are happening. Learning to praise the practices you really believe in is an art and Jesus shows us how. Jesus has another busy schedule. He agrees to divert and go to the centurion's house. More pressure. And then the break, the shaft of brilliant insight and commitment and Jesus picks up on it like lightning.

At the other end of the spectrum is Jesus' criticism of Peter for trying to dissuade him from the cross (Matt 16:21-28). When we measure what Peter said against what we know about him, we are almost offended by the ferocity and personal nature of Jesus' attack. We feel that Jesus should look beyond the advice to the spirit in which it was given (perhaps even then, Peter deserved what he got), but Jesus senses something so much more serious. This undermines the whole reason he came to earth. His mission, his plans, all the mental and spiritual preparation he has been putting into that moment from the time he first learned to think, is being written off.

Surely there is a lesson here in leadership. But the lesson is not about being outspoken. It is about being aware of what is really important. We can apply it with our kids. Is it more important that they eat stylishly, or that they eat heartily and healthily? Which will we commend and make a fuss over? Is it more important that they learn the value of their money or that they learn to give? Given a limited time to influence them, will we commend a moment of thoughtless generosity, or complain about pennies wasted on sweets or bits of plastic? And how does this apply to training the grown-up kids in church?

Taking the negative stance properly is more difficult. We may remember harsh words spoken in church meetings. Some will recall sombre speakings from the pulpit about people no longer in the pews (or even more uncomfortably, about the current occupants). A general dread of those moments seems to linger in our corporate memory, leaving a strong distaste for any forthrightness at all. I suppose the nearest I can get by way of example was my Dad's sensitivity to certain 'attitudes'. Now that I am a Dad myself, I find I notice those arrogant gestures that squeeze the sincerity out of an apology or transform an innocent enquiry into a barefaced challenge. I sometimes find myself reacting more to those than to the original incident.

Perhaps the best known 'stop the world' incident is one that Matthew relates, but without the tension that Mark and Luke describe (Matt 9:20-22; Mark 5:24-34; Luke 8:43-48). Ironically, we are nearer to the ward round, too, with a woman sneaking up for healing and Jesus working his way around the immediate crowd, trying to work out what has happened. The disciples do not get it at all, jostled as they are from all sides. Again, the incident spawns more questions that we can address here. Doesn't Jesus know who has reached out? Surely he would have known the sensitivities of the situation! Does he want people to understand the difference between miracles and magic – that you are not healed by accident? Will that second in the public eye make it easier for the woman to take the next steps and be fully integrated back into her society (see Lev 15:25-30)?

Who knows? But for some reason, Jesus holds up the crowd. And we break from this encounter with a vivid picture of a shy woman who had a horribly embarrassing problem, who has run out of answers and makes her way to Jesus. We discover that the issue which dominated her days was not too big for Jesus, that she did not have to force her way into his schedule or demand an audience, that Jesus did not have to gather all his resources and concentrate like crazy for this one. And faith is like that, driving us to the little actions that you could easily miss in the rough and tumble of the crowd, but triggering the most amazing cascades of blessing.

She leaves the encounter knowing that the blessing has been given freely. She has not stolen her healing from a grudging providence. Jesus is glad she has been healed. He wants her to go in peace. It's all OK.

And how else would we have known if Jesus had not stopped the world?

I remember a story that went something like this. A city boy was walking through New York with a Native American. All at once, the Native American grabbed his arm and said he could hear a cricket (would that be right?). Anyway, after some searching around, he found the insect and held it up. The city boy was astonished at such acute hearing and started to go on about it, but was stopped by the Native American who flicked a nickel into the air. As it hit the sidewalk, half a dozen heads turned. I do not know how much of the story I have got right there, but just try flicking a coin in a crowd.

As a stranger in our world, Jesus has a different set of values – he hears and sees things differently. As Christians we, too, are learning to live with a new set of ears and eyes. One of the ways to help other Christians in this pursuit is to make a song and dance about the important things from that world whenever we come across them in this, however grey they may look at first, or however faintly they may chirrup to us.

Time for a parable

Meandering through Matthew again, we find Jesus launching into a parable when John's disciples ask about fasting (Matt 9:14-17). The burst wineskins, in particular, provide an enduring image of what he means by new. The parable enables Jesus to give a concise response, addressing the question and the crowd at the same time.

My favourite parable-from-a-question comes from Luke (12:13-21): a father's estate is dividing two brothers and the one who has lost out comes to Jesus to sort things out. The story has lots of intriguing angles. For us, with our current concerns for social justice, Jesus is surprisingly unwilling to intervene. Surely Jesus, of all people, could have acted fairly for the family. Whatever became of that brother? Could he have survived without any inheritance?

It is a powerful and emotive question. It has the crowd's attention. Imagine being asked the question yourself. How would you handle it? Is this chap a perennial whinger? What are the most important issues?

Jesus takes a surprising stance. He comes from a world where affluence is less than paper thin. There are things in that world that matter, really matter, but money is not one of them. Security and freedom from worry, however, do matter – even in Jesus' world. How can he make the crowd understand how radically different his world is from theirs? How can he help them to understand it, to feel it, to get so close to the concept that they are in serious danger of believing it?

After briefly disengaging from the personal call to arbitrate, Jesus focuses on money, firstly in a negative way and then (if the petitioner was still around) in a positive way.

The parable of the rich fool is a whizzo parable. Working on the fly, Jesus deftly sketches out the ample frame of a successful farmer. The picture of such prosperity must have left a profound impression on the impecunious man in the crowd. And it goes on getting better. And then, in one of those twists characteristic of so many parables, Jesus throws the whole thing up the air. The pizza that takes up so much of the work surface, looks terribly fragile as the pizzaola flings it up in the air. And so it is for our farmer. Someone else is watching proceedings. Someone is in the wings, and from that perspective, all this opulence is wafer thin. His soul! His soul was what really mattered, and he had not even considered it. The crowd had not considered it. Nor had we.

But Jesus does not leave it there. This chap needs security. The crowd needs security. Jesus' world is a wonderfully safe world.

So Jesus moves on in his teaching (Luke 12:22ff) to remind the crowd that God enjoys looking after those who cannot look after themselves. So Jesus has used the opportunity to drive home some important teaching. He has done this partly by warning the man whose cause we would naturally have taken. He develops this with a lively and relevant parable and then returns to the root of the chap's insecurity. How often are we willing to avoid the obvious answer in order to pursue the deeper issues?

The running commentary

Wherever we find Jesus with the crowd, it is not long before he is commenting on something that has happened. It is remarkable that he can do this without losing his audience – then or now. Most people who feel the need to comment on everything strike us as either pompous or boring. But not here. The crowds mill and swell, press, surge and do all they can to hear more.

Jesus clearly believes there is an amazing range of things that his audience will never discover left to itself. He will make the communication as striking and memorable as he can – and he really can! But he must inject something into their view.

If we dodge back in Matthew to the encounter with John the Baptist's disciples (11:1-19), Jesus answers their question and then, as they are leaving, addresses the crowd about John. Even now, with our understanding of God's plans, which nobody in the crowd could have imagined, Jesus is perplexing. The Pharisees and teachers of the law want a miracle (Matt 12:38). Jesus decides they need some teaching (Matt 12:39-45) and alludes to Jonah, Nineveh, Solomon, the Queen of the South, and most surprisingly of all, provides teaching on demon possession. Someone has a quiet word with Jesus as he addresses the crowd: his family want to see him (Matt 12:46-50). Jesus takes the opportunity to say something about the family that really belongs to him. We never find out whether he went off to see them.

These are only examples but they seem pretty typical. It is hard to imagine the impact of such a torrent of teaching on anyone who followed Jesus for a reasonable time. We see something of the impression it left on the band of disciples. As Jesus coordinates this with the more searching, probing approach adopted in private, living around Jesus must have been a formidable experience. Jesus: alert to every nuance of a situation, focusing on a few basic truths, identifying them in situation after situation. Jesus: illustrating his ideas in the dusty, jostling, tiring fabric of a day with the crowd.

I remember reading a story about a chess team from a very underprivileged part of the world. It may have been the Bronx. It told how success in chess had transformed the characters who made up the team. The incident that sticks in my mind was the first time they were treated to a restaurant meal together. Menus were foreign territory to the team. Their teacher soon sensed their unease and wisely began to talk his own way through the menu, reasoning aloud how he planned to make his selection. A team bright enough to win tournaments soon caught on and their embarrassment was averted.

In a sense, Jesus is doing this. He is not simply going to reason with people. He is not content merely to teach the crowd (although we have to come back to that, because the leaders he produced clearly embraced that teaching). He wants people to trace the thinking through. He wants them to understand that, as he reveals God as Father, it implies a set of family relationships forged of stronger stuff than anything we can build relationships with in our world. He wants them to understand that his teaching on money is neither idealistic, nor designed to ease the struggle or sense of injustice in a world where there is rarely enough to go around. He lived pretty much without it, challenged people about it, told parables about it, because he really didn't think it mattered all that much. More importantly, he knew that our innate belief that it matters a lot is very dangerous.

For me, the intriguing thing about this is that people wanted to get close to Jesus. Living with those who will challenge everything you say is difficult. I have come across it on training courses – where you can bear it for a few days. You learn something about yourself but often the short-term result is that you simply learn to adapt the way you say things so as to avoid being challenged all the time. I know a few people who will challenge me regularly. At times they can be very helpful, but I confess I find it hard to love them all the time. I know a lot of people find me too challenging and find it hard to love me all the time. And I do not blame them.

Why was Jesus different? Was it because he had time for them? Was it because the miracles were so spectacular that they made up for any amount of personal discomfort? Was it because the Holy Spirit helped things to fit into place for those who tried to see things through Jesus' eyes?

Formal teaching

A friend of mine was coming to the end of his stretch with a Christian student organization and was wondering what to do next. He wanted to become a pastor somewhere, and he tried to tell me why. In the end, he sort of gave up and told me he just had to preach. And now he is a pastor with a real gift in teaching.

Luke introduces Jesus, fresh from his initiation of baptism and temptation, reading out the lesson in the local synagogue. What is the reading? 'The Spirit of the Lord is upon me, because he has anointed me to preach good news to the poor...' (Luke 4:18). Time and again, Jesus' reaction to a crowd, as well as healing its sick, is to teach. Mark specifically links Jesus' response in teaching to his compassion for the crowd (Mark 6:34). What can he do for all these needy, worried, helpless people? He can teach them.

I said at the start that Jesus did not run a Sabbath school. That is only partly true, since Jesus' teaching provides the academic backdrop to all his students learned, did, or experienced on the road with him. Teaching the crowds, parables for the crowd, interaction with the crowd. Day in, day out.

Enigma variations

So what was Jesus' teaching like? Well, enigmatic. It was deliberately obscure and, when you try to get into it yourself you find it elusive in practice. 'But to those on the outside everything is said in parables so that, "they may be ever seeing but never perceiving, and ever hearing but never understanding"' (Mark 4:11,12). Try to take some of the best known of Jesus teaching: The Beatitudes (Matt 5:1-12). Where is the world where the poor in spirit are blessed? Is it in our world? Is it in heaven? Is it in the church? Is it an aspirational sort blessing – that they ought to be blessed? When you first hear it, it sounds wonderful. As you try to take it apart it becomes more and more complex. Many attempts to make sense of the passage seem to me (and I haven't covered them all) to need a shoehorn and axle grease to fit the concept of poor in spirit into being blessed or vice versa.

Personally, I find it easier to pick out one that makes some sense even in my world – perhaps the merciful being shown mercy – work around that and then pick off the next most difficult. With time and meditation you can get to a place where they make sense, where they point to a lifestyle and a walk with God that is truly fulfilling and even possible in this world. But it doesn't come easily.

Now why does Jesus who wants so much to teach the crowds adopt this perplexing approach? There are zillions of possible reasons. Fortunately we have an agenda in looking at Jesus' training methods, and that provides a focus to the question. What effect would this type of teaching have had on the next generation of leaders?

My favourite physics teacher was a chap called Richard Feynmann, not that I ever heard him lecture. I had to read the books. One chapter in volume II of his lectures on physics is essentially a verbatim record of a complete session. In it he sets out to explain a principle which he exploited time and again throughout his life. It is called the Principle of Least Action (which sounds like it might appeal to a mathematician or physicist) and basically it represents a massive short cut in a huge range of problems which you might tackle. It is an elegant way of standing back from all the detail and still getting a complete answer.

He begins by explaining how he came across it. His teacher, recognising that he was a bright boy, showed him the start of the secret – and then left him to it. He goes on to explain that his teacher was a great teacher, but that his audience does not have such a good teacher, so he will introduce the secret and go on to explain it. What follows is fabulous physics. The paradox is which of the two was the better teacher. Was it his teacher who recognised a brilliant student and just opened the box enough to let him peep in and see the mystery, or was it Feynmann, thrilling the crowd with a virtuoso performance?

In a sense, Jesus sets out his stall as Feynmann's teacher did. He wants to attract those who will go away and think about it. He wants to give them enough to last them a lifetime. He wants them to grasp principles that they can apply over and over again. He wants them to understand, not because they have been told, but because they have been part of the process. They have discovered something in the teaching for themselves. He wants them to ponder, to get excited, to run the themes through the fingers of their soul for sheer joy.

I always feel as if John has done just that. The way in which ideas recur throughout his gospel and letters, reinforced in repetition, gives me the impression that he has taken the teaching away and gone through it time and again. As one of the younger disciples, perhaps the youngest, the teaching might be expected to have made the most profound impact on him anyway. Seven times in chapters 2 and 3 of Revelation we have an echo of Jesus' own encouragement, 'He who has an ear…'

Note that Jesus' teaching is not wishy-washy. It is not a set of riddles. We will explore the simplicity of it later. It is not wrapped up in code to avoid censure – rather like a dissident playwright under a harsh regime might resort to allegory or key words. Jesus is far too direct at other times for that explanation to work. Having said that, there is the little postscript to the parable of the tenants (Matt 21:33-44). 'When the chief priests and the Pharisees heard Jesus' parables, they knew he was talking about them' (v 45).

It does not actually say that they understood the parables but they just knew they were being referred to. So what is Jesus doing? He is quite explicit in Matthew 11:25, 'I praise you, Father, Lord of heaven and earth, because you have hidden these things from the wise and learned and revealed them to little children.' So Jesus has found a way of teaching which discriminates against the disinterested and against those who rely on their intellect to decipher it.

Is this a sensible way to train leaders today? Surely there are enough attractions, distractions and downright important things for potential leaders to do, without adding new hurdles. Surely they need their teaching cut and dried – there on the plate with no messing. Get it into them! Life is confusing enough. Make it all dead plain, and drive it home dynamically. Tell them what to do in each and every situation.

I like to draw a distinction between training and education. Training teaches you what to do while education teaches you how to think. You want to work a piece of equipment? You get trained. The next generation of kit comes along and you need a training boost to operate that. There are all kinds of health, safety and legal drivers pushing us this way but we are in danger of becoming the most highly trained generation ever with a seriously eroded capability to think at all. And what happens in the workplace will happen at church.

One of the unexpected benefits of the proliferation of Bible translations has been the move away from 'proof' texts. When everyone used the same translation, you found the verse that dealt with an issue unambiguously and that was that. Now it is different. The verse does not quite close the matter in everyone's translation. At first sight this is disastrous. Suddenly there is no absolute truth. As usual, however, God has not left his people without guidance. He just expects them to work a little harder. Most of the proof texts were actually right in the truth they were identifying. However, now you must find the truth by applying the whole weight of scripture. The result is actually more satisfying. The truth is more secure, because you have to work it from so many more angles. And you have understood the whole, rather than argued from a part. Sadly, we have failed to benefit from this blessing in disguise because we have largely failed to engage with the whole book.

But Jesus' teaching is like that. He has not come to fill his kingdom with either Smart Alecs, or automatons. Intellect will not be a barrier, but intellectual arrogance will, and the key to the gate is a humble interest in what he has to say: 'He who has ears, let him hear' (e.g. Matt 13:9).

So how do we teach enigmatically? How do we infuse that degree of mystery into our talks so that people are challenged to think it through with enough hope for them not to give up too soon? Here comes the great cop out: I cannot write it down in a few paragraphs. If I could, you could pick up the technique without having to think about it. The golden rule is that you cannot pass on something thoughtful if you have not had to wrestle with it yourself.

But there are some clues. Abandon all preparation that seeks for three easy points in the passage. In any case, half the audience will see points two and three coming long before you get there. If you find the passage tricky, try to convey something of that in your talk. Describe the questions it raises in your mind. Take your listeners through the process by which you have arrived at what you believe it to mean. Do not be afraid of looking like an idiot. I remember a lecturer once saying that you were not ignorant according to what you did not know. You were ignorant according to what you did know – that wasn't true! Try to work out how the truth you are discovering might impact on your life – and explore some of the ways it might affect theirs. The really great secret in all this is that the Bible is wonderfully enigmatic. You do not have to work it up. It is already there, waiting for you as you seek to teach it.

Get this!

Enigmatic? Evangelistic. Jesus is always proclaiming, preaching, thrusting. So much of the content of his talks is dedicated to describing different worlds – heaven and hell. We hear of wheat that is gathered into barns while the weeds are burned, Lazarus with Abraham while the rich man is in torment, people who cut off limbs and gouge out eyes in order to escape a fate worse than death, prudent investors who inherit cities, and the totally undeserving who make it to the banquet in the end. Even the time Jesus puts into teaching about life on earth is about a different life. Wineskins that cannot take the swell, buildings that withstand the flood, a despised foreigner looking after the chap who has just been mugged.

Jesus has an agenda for change mediated by individuals realizing that they have to make a decision. People should be worried about the prospects if they do not change. People should get excited about the prospects if they do. People should stop living by the principles they have adopted to date and start off with a new set of priorities. The agenda for change is one of the last things Jesus passes on to his disciples as he leaves them. You may listen through Matthew's ears at the Ascension ('Therefore, go and make disciples of all nations, baptising them in the name of the Father and of the Son and of the Holy Spirit, and teaching them to obey everything I have commanded you.' Matt 28:19,20) or with John on that first Easter Sunday ('As the Father has sent me, I am sending you.' John 20:21). The message is the same. Jesus has a message to proclaim. We all know what that is. Our teaching is to be rich with it.

But doesn't too much talk about heaven and hell turn people off? It does not stop the insurance companies advertising. You know the scenarios. People younger than you have just retired to the most amazing yacht, sailing in serenest seas. Friendly dolphins pop up to congratulate them on their astute choice of pension provider. Mrs Jones, a haggard unfortunate, sits in a damp flat telephoning her friends to borrow a tin of baked beans.

Sadly, her husband had not availed himself of an appropriate insurance product before he was attacked by a swarm of killer bees while inadvertently applying honey instead of creosote to the fence. Media images designed to attract, frighten, stop us in our tracks, or encourage us to plan for a better future. They are not afraid to drive home a message that what you do or forget to do today can affect your tomorrow.

It is probably this aspect of Jesus' own ministry that is most strongly reflected in the preaching of those he trained. They brandished this message, enthusiastically, often forcefully, and with an accent on the consequences of rejecting it. They made it appeal, they showed it was relevant, they argued, cajoled, persuaded and proclaimed. As the Holy Spirit delivers an explosive response in the form of thousands of conversions, the sharp weapon of attack is the message, handled by the people Jesus had trained in the way he had trained them to use it.

And today? Is it possible to teach about heaven and hell, to talk of eternity and to do so in relevant terms, in ways that will capture attention and drill through to people's wills? I think heaven is easier to talk about than hell – and maybe that is the place to start. Somehow, if we believe anything at all about what Jesus taught, we need to drag ourselves away from the inexorable tendency to believe that this life is all that matters. That belief will overwhelm us. Even those of us who affirm the doctrine of an afterlife need close encounters with God's word on the topic to switch us out of our malaise. Perhaps the most positive step we can take is to schedule these topics into our teaching plans. There is nothing like having a topic and knowing your congregation, to focus the mind on the business of communicating something meaningfully.

Anyway, Jesus did it, and his disciples learnt to do so too.

You don't have to listen to this

In one sense, a crowd is the ultimate expression of democracy. You don't have to stand and listen. There are a million ways to drift off if it gets boring. Football crowds, having paid a small fortune for the privilege of watching and cheering, have a curious way of drifting off with ten minutes to spare with the home side 3-0 down and the rain tipping down as well. Crowds stay and listen because they want to.

And they wanted to listen to Jesus. Why? Well, presumably, his talks excited them, answered their needs and encouraged them that there was help at hand for their struggle into the kingdom. Clearly there were other things to draw the crowds who were hungry for healing, miracles, spectacle. There were times when it must have been nice to hear the religious rulers, with their apparent stranglehold on the gates of the kingdom, being given a verbal lashing. But when all was said and done, they stayed and listened to the teaching.

So much has been written about how Jesus taught that we cannot contribute anything significant here. Even when we have piled up all our scholarship, however, it is hard to grasp the excitement that ran along the edges of the crowds, pulses of surprise pumping through it, the amazement, the gladness and at times the fear, and the rippling sense of something new that ran along behind him and crushed up close to him whenever he stopped.

Jesus told bright, sturdy stories, sketching them with confidence, mixing and matching them as the occasion demanded. Scary things happen to people in Jesus' stories. They die but can look right into Abraham's lap from their place in the pit (Luke 16:19-31). They manage to sneak into a party that was open to everyone anyway, only to be confronted by an angry host who pitches them out again (Matt 22:1-14). They fail to stock up on oil and miss out on the wedding banquet (Matt 25:1-13). Strange things happen to them. After the most grossly insulting behaviour culminating in senseless dissipation of half the family fortune, they hit rock bottom, screw up all their humility and return home to the staggering surprise of frank forgiveness (Luke 15:11-32). A dodgy manager finds his contract terminated but receives a personal commendation for his perceptive response to unemployment (Luke 16:1-9). Wonderful things happen too. Someone busts a gut to double his master's investment in him and walks into a life of luxury and responsibility (Matt 25:14-30).

People make strange decisions in Jesus' stories. They sell up to wander around with a pearl (Matt 13:45,46). And those making sensible decisions find themselves unexpectedly called to account for their short sightedness (Luke 12:13-21). However you look at Jesus' teaching it was wonderfully woven. You would have stood and listened for hours, too.

To me, the amazing thing is the way in which Jesus serves up this combination without the hours of preparation. I guess there had been a lifetime of preparation, and we have already noted Jesus making time to get away. But so much of Jesus' ministry is thrown together quickly, extemporaneously, sure-footedly.

I guess the message is obvious. However difficult we may find it, people will listen if we have an interesting way of saying it. A boring approach will see thinning crowds even when the material is vital to them. Have you ever read the safety manual at work? Through? From cover to cover?

Is there a recipe for relevant, content-packed teaching? I went to a friend's fortieth birthday party the other day. His wife had made it child-friendly and, as part of the package, had hired a children's entertainer. The chap was exceptionally good – all kinds of little tricks that turned a magic show into an event. He was so good that most of the adults stood and watched too, giggling surreptitiously and generally enjoying the show. Towards the end, he did a trick in which he joined two pieces of string together. One of my sons was really caught by this and continued to inspect the string while the entertainer wrapped up the show. When they realised he was about to go, there was this clamour to know how he did it – and he told them. He said they should go to their rooms, stand in front of the mirror and practice for fourteen years. And then they would know how to do the trick.

Exciting teaching is hard. It demands the time to work out what the text told them then and is telling us now. It means struggling with illustrations that are relevant to the audience and to the passage. It means finding the best stories in your own failures. It means spiritual exercise and development of gift. It means a relentless willingness to recognise how it could have been done better last time and must be done better next time.

But the results are top.

Easy does it

Finally, Jesus' teaching was easy. The ordinary people flocked to hear Jesus. Mark reports, 'The large crowd listened with delight' (Mark 12:37). And the intelligentsia despised them for it. Remember the temple guards sent to arrest Jesus in John 7 (vv 32, 45-52)? They return empty handed, reporting that no-one spoke the way Jesus did. What? Have they been deceived, too? Have any of the Pharisees believed in Jesus? 'But this mob that knows nothing of the law – there is a curse on them.'

So if Jesus taught things that were too enigmatic for the clever people, what was it that was easy for everyday people? Well, you don't have to be a genius to realise that Jesus was rather keen on the kingdom of God. It was quietly growing all around, it had insignificant beginnings, but would dominate the land-scape one day, it was worth giving up all you had for, it was populated with people who were meek, peace-loving, poor in spirit. How did you get there? You followed Jesus!

Where did Jesus stand on love? Did you just love your friends? How often should you forgive your friends? How should you sort out a relationship when it went bad? What about loving your wife? Was Jesus keen on divorce? How about loving God? How much effort and energy did Jesus expect the exercise to consume? The answers are not very difficult. And this is part of the wonder of Jesus' teaching: the individual bits can get quite complicated. Jesus' teaching can be horribly con-fusing or wonderfully stimulating depending on whether you are trying to force it open intellectually or to take it by faith. But the broad brush strokes are really rather plain. I suppose it is a bit like an impressionist painting. From a distance it is pretty clear. It is the clash of colour and shape at the finer level that makes it unacceptable to some and fascinating to others.

And perhaps it is worth making a plea for more big picture teaching. We get hold of a book of the Bible, split it into twenty sections of 35 verses each, remove the tricky passages and then ask a visiting speaker to handle 16.38 verses this week. We won-der why people get lost in the labyrinthine analysis. Why does it fail to excite them? Why are they unable to link this week's teaching to last week's? Ironically, with all the study aids, mes-sages, videos, and application notes, we seem to have a genera-tion which has very little idea of what the Bible as a whole says. We seem to have spent so much time trying to read between the lines that we have lost any idea of what the lines themselves say.

Big picture teaching. Sure there will be times when you have to drill down. I am not pretending that divorce is an easy topic. But deciding whether it is allowed and if so, when, is a very dif-ferent matter from working out whether Jesus was in favour of it or not. Big picture teaching gives a sense of perspective.

Increasingly we make decisions on the balance of local pressures. Big picture teaching helps us to know what God wants overall. It helps us to know whether the decision we are making is in line with those principles, an exception to the rules, or contrary to them.

This is not a very good way of putting it, but you know you have effective big picture teaching when regulars in the congregation develop a sort of spiritual intuition. They may not be able to prove their view but they have a consistent set of convictions about what is a good idea and what is not. On the other hand, the person who will argue from the detail in each situation, often very persuasively but unpredictably, may well lack the big picture teaching. It is a tricky line to draw. However, Jesus' ministry shows the importance of living on the right side of it.

In summary

As well as interactive teaching, Jesus is prepared to stand up and say what he believes. Jesus is into content. The gospel writers report swathes of solid, engaging teaching. Jesus takes opportunities on the road, in front of a crowd, wherever, to bring his teaching home. The relentlessness of his teaching, its variety in terms of argument, parable, example and advice, make Jesus' teaching sharp and incisive two thousand years later. And it proved an effective tool for training the next generation of leaders.

In a sense our task is much easier. We have the content. Scripture is jam-packed full of it. And Jesus has left us with a great example of how to pick it up and fling it into the crowd.

Thinking it through

1. How do Jesus' parables on fields and gardens support his training initiatives in evangelism?
2. What differences between Jesus' world and ours show up when he overhears the Pharisees and teachers of the law complaining about his associations with sinners (see Luke 15)?
3. To what extent should condemnation of religious leaders (e.g. Luke 11:37-54) feature in our teaching today?

4. What style of teaching grabs our generation's interest in the way that parables attracted Jesus' audiences? What worked fifty years ago? A hundred years ago?

5. As you are giving out the notices, someone pipes up about the state the kitchen was left in last Friday night. You want to extract teaching value from the encounter. What might you do?

6. List three of the best and three of the worst things about public ministry in church as compared to Jesus' teaching.

7. What elements of Jesus' public teaching about money do we see reflected in the early church's behaviour?

8. List ten topics from Jesus' teaching which are important today and rank them according to how easy or difficult they are to communicate.

6

Me? A Mentor?

Involved in any Christian service? Who will do it when you're gone?

If anyone was irreplaceable, it was Jesus. And there were things he knew only he could do. Redemption, salvation, and sending the Holy Spirit were things he could not pass on to someone else. But the weirdest thing is that Jesus, with a tight timetable and a unique ministry, is keen to train successors.

Most of the time, it is bad news to train your successor. You may find yourself out of a job. Someone we know was told to train a successor if he wanted promotion. He did, and was made redundant. His old employer had a newly trained, lower cost alternative. We need to be indispensable.

Do the same insecurities creep into our church life? Who knows, our successor might be better than we are. People might like the new face better. People will not value us if we are not doing something vital. Could we ever learn to do something else?

Apart from the clergy, missionaries and the odd full-time worker, Christian service tends to be done by workers who took on the task without much preparation and relinquish it reluctantly. Strangely enough, the scene is chronically short of people, too. Are the two related?

Jesus knows he has little time, trains his followers and leaves them to it. They go out and, once they get the hang of things, the pattern is repeated. Churches are formed, leaders appointed and the founders move on. Even leadership of the church in Jerusalem appears to fall to James who had not been one of the twelve disciples.

Stuck in a rut? What would you like to do next?

Fortunately, mentoring addresses both ends of the service spectrum. At the start, it delivers a stream of disciples, providing them with a way to find their gifts, to develop appropriate skills and to enter service. They are ready for service when they begin and can operate with confidence, initially in a secure environment. At the other end, people in service have trained successors, au fait with the system and ready to inject new energy and ideas into the situation. And good mentors can move on to new things.

I enjoy speaking. But I am finding that I get at least as much of a kick out of working with a team, and getting the team to do the speaking. It is nice when someone comes up to you after a talk and says how much they enjoyed what you said. I usually ask them exactly what it was that they enjoyed. That gives you some insight into how well you are getting your ideas across. Sometimes it is a little depressing. Maybe they think you have a cute accent. But to work with a team over several weeks, to see the individuals grasp ideas, explore them and shape them into communicable material – that is wonderfully rewarding. And there is much less uncertainty about what it is that has been learned through the exercise.

Mentors can have great fun. If they manage to work themselves out of a job, there are loads of new things to try. But often the doors will only open to those with the courage to train themselves out of a job.

Too much to do? Who can you call on for help?

Mentoring spreads the workload even during training. It is a people multiplier. When Jesus sends out the Twelve, or again, the six dozen (Luke 9 and 10) presumably villages are evangelized that Jesus never has time to visit. It is a training exercise and a successful mission all in one. Industrialists report dramatic improvements in productivity while process improvement initiatives are underway. It worked in one context then – it works now in others. I am working with a team on Galatians. They presented their introduction to Galatians at our church last Sunday. They received excellent reviews (I should tell you that our church is really good at encouraging this type of thing, so rave reviews do not mean it was perfect). If you are ever a reader of this, next Sunday will be in the distant past. However, it is their turn again this coming week looking at freedom and rules. On both occasions, I have had engagements elsewhere.

Hey! We have a multiplier on our hands. It is not quite as miraculous as it sounds, because while the team has some people for whom the study and delivery of a Sunday morning's worth of content is new, others have brought in some experience which had nothing to do with me. It was there anyway and it is helping the team. But still, we do not have to wait until the exercise is over to benefit from new speakers. We have already increased our capability here as a church.

Not enough capable people? Where will they come from?

All discipleship involves some sort of service. Mentoring provides development for everyone. And it provides better quality development because the training is in the context and setting in which the job must eventually be done, and provided by someone who has practical experience of the task. Commerce and industry are moving away from the lecture theatre and onto the project or even into role-play for their training, from the classroom to on-the-job development. Even residential courses now come with a hefty slice of work-oriented preparation and lead into projects based in the working environment. And it is not primarily to save money. It is to stop wasting money. The history of training is full of expensive courses that failed to make any impact beyond the following weekend.

The leader as trainer

People are waking up to the fact that the best person to train is the one doing the job already. The emergence of the leader-trainer is one of the sea changes in modern industrial development. In a recent interview, Jacques Nasser, CEO of Ford, describes how cascade training reached its 55,000 salaried employees around the world within 3 years to drive through its change programme. He trained the team around him and they trained their teams, and so forth. PepsiCo reached out to its workforce of 20,000 in 18 months. Noel Tichy, describes the approach in the *Harvard Business Review* (March/April '99) and notes: 'Great Leaders – be they of corporations, churches, or armies – have probably been using it forever.' I can't comment on corporations or armies, but if we are talking about the church...

We have taken a very quick look at the emphasis Jesus placed on training his disciples. Jesus was not after a bunch of followers to gain credibility. He took them and gave them the best training he could. He did not need a group of people to look after him and ease his passage through life. He decided to look after them so that when he was gone, they could look after others. Presumably because of the literature left to us, we see this most clearly as Paul trains Timothy, encouraging and challenging him to make his mark as a leader, to take the gospel which Paul received and hand it on, untarnished, vital and viable, to the next generation.

Who might it work for?

I guess everyone has a hunch that it might work for the vicar, pastor, parson, minister, full-time elder, or whatever you have in your church, fellowship, chapel, assembly or whatever. And we need to come back to this group.

But we will miss the big opportunity if we see this as another task for our full-timers. You are a young people's leader. How long have you been leading? How long do you plan to continue? Who is lined up to take over? You have run a home group for the past five years. Who will run it for the next five? You launched and ran the most successful series of men's events your church has ever seen. Who is going to take it on and reap a harvest of real men getting saved? You are up to your neck in Toddlers or Pre-school for the church. You are struggling to feed 75 senior citizens at your weekly lunch club, you look after the crèche on Sunday mornings, you are the audio expert, you manage the tape library, you have created a resource centre, you this, you that… You are exhausted and you will not be around forever.

You might even long to do something different. Not all longing is wrong. You may have gifts that you suspect are not being used because you are too busy already. There is that lovely verse in Hosea, where God urges his people: 'Break up your fallow ground' (Hos 10:12, AV). Going back to things that have lain dormant for years can be wonderfully refreshing. But perhaps there are things you have never done before. Perhaps you would like to join the worship band or chorus. Perhaps you have a burden to beautify the building with wall hangings. Perhaps you would like to get some support behind the couple who sold up to spend the rest of their lives in another part of the world serving Jesus. Perhaps you feel called to spend more time praying, or meditating, or studying, or just enjoying the presence of God.

And what about the pastors, vicars or ministers? It is a weird sort of existence, isn't it? Part of the body. Part of something meant to be rich in relationships, yet left to plough a lonely furrow so much of the time. I guess part of this is self-inflicted.

However much we seek for balance in our candidates or the ministry teams they join, most pastors enjoy preparing and speaking. Most have a real gift in this area. And for most, a great deal of their time and energy goes into the preaching and teaching.

I remember being told that the first half of a job always took 90% of the time and the second half took the other 90%. It's a bit like that in full-time service. A large chunk of effort goes into preparation, another 90% goes into pastoral work, another 90% goes into community relations – and so forth. Would this sort of approach, this leader-as-trainer, this effort-multiplying, offer something? Would more people develop gifts if the pulpit were shared around a bit more? Can one still take responsibility for the quality of teaching without actually delivering the teaching? I think you can, and I believe Jesus gave a very clear lead on how to set about it.

How can I go about mentoring?

I guess there might be two groups of people asking this question. Overworked leaders, who have to run everything might grasp this as an opportunity. At the other end of the leadership spectrum may be those who have never really valued their role in the scheme of things, and would ordinarily have lacked the courage to stand up and ask for people to follow where they have trodden. Either group could struggle. The leader-from-the-front may tend to dominate proceedings and lose the team. Team members get frustrated because they do not really buy into what is happening or just get depressed about ever being let loose on their own. The lone operator, on the other hand, emerging into the glare of a team's expectations, may lack the confidence to take the team forward.

How many failures?

And I do not know the answers. I suspect you have to find out the answers for yourself. What I can do is pass on some of my successes and failures in hope that you will be encouraged to experiment for yourself. And our failures are important. I love reading Robert Sheehan in *The Times*. He writes the bridge column and must be a very good player to hold such a position. I say, 'must be' because I am not good enough to know. I learned to play bridge a few years ago and never really reached beginner level. That is not modesty – I just cannot get the guessing side of the game. Anyhow, I read bridge columns in the hope that something will rub off on me. If Robert Sheehan reports a hand he has played, it is almost always one he has messed up.

I like Robert. Preposterous as it sounds, I leave his column with the impression that I might not be shown up too badly were I to play with him. I feel I can learn something about bridge with Robert. And, in my experience, having a go at involving people will be an experience rich in failure. Even the things you thought went well leave a little story, which surfaces later, of dissatisfaction, neglect or unfulfilled ambition. But what matters most, the five failures or the time when everything really worked together? Do strikers worry about the dozens of wild shots, spectacular misses at short range, volley attempts which miss the ball (to say nothing of the net) or the couple of goals every few games which go in? Even then, not all the goals are attractive. There are the mad scrambles where you were the last to touch the ball, the defensive disasters, and the flukes as well as the spectacular set pieces, overhead bicycle kicks and reflex strokes of genius that you remember for a lifetime.

Just over a week ago I watched the second half of Manchester United's victory over Bayern Munich. I was in a room full of serious United fans who were wilting in desperation as their team seemed doomed to miss out on the treble. I am at the couch potato end of the armchair critic spectrum but I noticed that the team was setting up chances. They were not connecting but I reasoned that they could not go on failing forever. I like to think it was cold logic, but it was probably sheer contrariness that had me coolly predicting a United goal (and ultimate victory) as we entered the last couple of minutes of normal time. I made a name for myself with the little crowd of footballing cognoscenti that evening as United ascended the podium – although I certainly had no expectation of victory within normal time.

Basically, I don't believe you can go on failing forever. And the rewards of getting it right in the end are wonderful. Failures can also be rewarding if you take something forward into the next try.

I am not sure that we know immediately after a failure what

went wrong. One of the most exciting bits of evangelism my wife and I got involved in was with another couple in following up two other couples from a Billy Graham campaign. The material we ended up using was not the prescribed stuff, but after a hesitant start the eight of us got on like a house on fire. We did not know where each of the four starters were when we started out, but after weeks of late (Thursday) nights, they both joined (other) churches and are still going strong. It was great fun. They enjoyed it. We enjoyed it. They learned new things and we wrestled with what the Bible said about the practical issues they raised.

I thought to myself that there was really nothing to this evangelism stuff. If you could get a discussion group, it would all flow. We went on to another enquirers-type study and it didn't work at all. It didn't work for us or for them. Everyone was very patient and kind about it, but nothing really clicked. Looking back, I think I tried to foist my ideas onto the rest of the team without really finding out what they wanted, whether they wanted it to be an enquirers' or a discipleship event. But even out of that there was some success. Another church borrowed the material and had fun with it.

I guess trying too hard to set the agenda and pace is one of my problems. I had wanted for ages to use teaching teams as a vehicle for developing new talent. I prepared outlines of the talks, templates for the acetates and held introductory meetings to explain the agenda. We had some good series, but I never saw them develop in the exciting way I vaguely imagined possible. You may find that sort of calamity befalls your efforts, too.

For what they are worth, here are some of my discoveries. I offer them, not because they are the best illustrations, but because most of them happened to me. If they can happen to me then they can happen to you, too. I just want to encourage you to have a go, building up your own stories of failure and success along the way.

Setting the agenda

One of the things that used to impress me about management training events was how much you got through without ever seeming to really rush. I had been on the receiving end of a really good programme and wondered whether engineers could

plan and get as much out of this way of doing things as the con-
sultants overseeing the course. I arranged to spend a day with
one of the course tutors. I had a specific type of event to plan
and I had done some thinking.

After the usual preamble, and some time spent going over the
aims of the event, he asked me what the objectives were. I
thought that aims and objectives were the same thing.

The most helpful thing I ever learned about teams was that
aims are not objectives. Aims can be quite general, objectives are
specific. Your aim may be for your Sunday school class to
understand Matthew better. Your objective for each student
might be that he or she be able to relate six parables from
Matthew and give one modern application for each. Your aim
might be to study Galatians together. Your objective might be to
produce and deliver four half-hour sessions to a family group of
mixed spiritual background. Your aim might be to enthuse the
congregation about mission. Your objective might be to persuade each family group represented to write to one missionary
within a month.

Having a clear set of aims and objectives is very important. I
like to write them down at work and I sometimes write them
down for church events. I ought to do so more. Clarity at the
start does two things. Firstly, it helps you to gain buy-in, as we
will see below. If you approach people to join in and they can
read what you want to achieve, they are more likely to turn up
with a set of aspirations that match other people's. Although
Jesus' disciples were not always clear about why they followed
him and got all muddled up over the restoration of the kingdom
of Israel, Jesus got them to the goal he promised at the start – the
fishermen became fishers of men.

The second thing a clear statement of what you hope to
achieve does, is that it enables you to set an agenda. You plan
backwards from the end. If you want your three teams to produce a T-shirt each on which they have written the ideal characteristics of a missionary on the front, and the key responsibilities
of the supporting church on the back, you work from there. It is
not just that you plan the time needed to do the T-shirt. You
need to plan how people will explore missionary gifts and training. Do you just want a list of the teams' prejudices or is there
going to be input from outside? How long will they have to
read, watch, listen, and discuss in order to reach an informed list

that involves everyone in learning something? Will you have to spend some time helping people to realise the importance of listening to others, or discovering how much material they already have access to, through atlases, newspapers, friends and the internet?

Often when I find myself starting to have deep philosophical debates with those around me about what we are up to, I realise that we have no clear agenda. It may not always be possible to have clarity. God often leads us a step at a time. But often our lack of clarity is because we have not thought it through beforehand.

Buy-in

I still find myself setting and then selling an agenda that others have not fully bought into. I have some responsibilities for booking speakers at our place. I like to discuss topics with the speakers, rather than just give them a slot in a series. Often in a spectrum of subjects, there will be something that a given speaker really cares about. However, I find myself getting all excited about some aspect of the discussion, publicising the talk on that basis, and then getting curious responses from everyone when the talk as delivered takes a quite different approach to the agreed title.

I think getting buy-in is hard. But it is not impossible. The first step is to realise whether you have people on your side or not. You can still make a success of something when people have not fully bought-in, but you have to realise that they have not fully bought in. Problems arise when you assume they have bought-in and they haven't.

So what is buy-in? Buy-in covers the things that everyone on the team can believe in. For instance, earlier on this year we needed an internet web site to represent our part of the company. I wanted to run it as a one-day exercise in which we assembled and wrote material, and built most of the web in a day using small teams so that we would have something by 5:00pm that would still require editing, but would be substantially the final product. I wrote out a specification for the day, stating what I thought we could achieve. As time went on, I began to realise that people who wanted the site didn't really believe we could get as far in a day as I thought we could. One by one, I had to work out with them why I thought we could get the whole thing done in one day. This was important, because if we were only going to bring text and pictures together (but not build a web site) the skills and computing resources we would have to assemble for the day would be very different. In the end, I did not get buy-in on how far we would get – but most people were prepared to have a go at actually building a prototype web site in a day. People who didn't like the idea of working 'live' with others looking over their shoulders, very generously agreed to give it a go. Their expectations were not as high as mine, but they were willing to try. And that was all the buy-in I could get. It was also all I needed, because they were as good as their word and worked magnificently to make a success of the day.

They actually had more fun than I did, because they produced much more than they imagined themselves capable of, while I fell just short of the target number of pages I had set for the day. They achieved something remarkable, and it all hinged on the way they were asked to do it. They understood what they were being asked to do, they wanted to achieve the final goal, and they were willing to give it a try.

Of course, even the most painstaking preparation will leave a few people uninspired. There was Judas among the Twelve. There will always be critics you cannot win over, reach an agreement with or cut down.

Again, so long as they are a minority, are allowed to voice their objections and are treated with respect, you can probably proceed. But your aim must be to achieve what you set out to achieve – not to win over the doubters. You may do that, but if you focus on the doubters you may lose on both fronts.

So how do you handle buy-in? The clear statement of objectives may be a self-selecting mechanism. Few people are sufficiently masochistic to join a team that wants to do something they do not. However, even if it is written down there is still scope for misunderstanding. A spoken summary carries more risk in this direction. You need to know whether you have buy-in.

Does everyone in the team want to take a set of morning services? Are they prepared to have a go when a role is identified for them? If they are not, it may not be the end of the world – you just need to know where you stand. We have had someone join our team on Galatians who explained from the start that it conflicted with another commitment so he could not join the team on the platform. We all understood that from the start and he has been a great blessing during our preparation sessions. More difficult is the chap who wants to work with the team, but isn't sure if he can commit himself to lead in prayer, or to prepare a sketch, or to read a slice of the epistle, or to sort out some acetates, or, in fact, to do anything specific.

If you have the buy-in, fine. If not, you need to talk it through. If your mentoring involves taking someone out to lead a service at which you have been asked to speak, and if they always want to prepare a short talk so that you are always left with ten minutes or less, you need to decide whether there is a way forward for you as a team. You may decide to switch and do the leading, or you may give up. Of course there will be times when people can be talked round. Maybe your apprentice for planning the men's events doesn't think it can work because five out of the last six events have been sporting ventures and he rather likes quiz nights. You might be able to reassure. Maybe your prospective successors as house group leaders assume you have to work with a particular publisher's material because that is what you have always used. Maybe they just need to know that they can choose the material themselves once they take over.

The point is that you need to know where people stand before you dive in. If it is a team job, you may be able to sort out misunderstandings one at a time, but it can all get a little hairy if four or five people start voicing objections just as you think you are ready for the off.

Finding a role

Perhaps one of the trickier aspects of all of this is finding a role for yourself. This problem actually stops most people from getting other people involved: why get someone else into the loop when it will take twice as long? Hey, twice as long to do what? If you are going to be a mentor, you need to be clear where your role begins and ends. If you want the job done in every detail as you would have done it yourself it will certainly take twice as long. If you can find a way to provide the overall vision and live with the way in which new people will implement that vision, it can be very rewarding.

I have just messed up here. A team I have been working with

has just hit its first less than brilliant Sunday morning. Bits were excellent, but they came away feeling that they had struggled. I thought they had struggled in places, too, and spent some time wondering why.

In the end I realised that I had set the agenda. I had decided what the key points were and they had tried to take them on and express them. As we had run out of time, I guess I was even more concerned that we get a couple of simple points over – but the team had not taken them on board. Now whether my analysis of what the key points were was right or wrong, the team clearly struggled to put across someone else's agenda. Next time I will try to back off and see what the team believes it can put across. Provided it isn't heresy and derives from the scriptures we are addressing, it is much better to run with what you can than to stumble with what you cannot.

So, are you going to facilitate, or evaluate? Motivate or dominate? It is hard to find a role, especially if the team looks to you as the expert – and in many cases, you may be mentoring for exactly that reason. Finding the right questions can be a great help under those circumstances.

Another way of finding a role is to decide what you want to learn. Having a clear idea of the things you want to learn can take that edge off your contribution, which might otherwise harden towards arrogance. It was easy for me in the internet web site exercise, because I wanted to find out about web technology. There were commercial artists and technical people there, so I did not have to get excited about style or content. I could focus on trying to pull it together and leave the (inevitable) struggle over style to others.

In an environment where some aspect of Bible study is central, you might well find yourself as the 'expert' to some degree. How can it be a learning experience for you, then? Surely your aim is to get as much as you know into the consciousness of the team! Well, you might like to learn how best to run exercises of that type. Be open with the team, and let them know what it is you are hoping to learn (and let them do the same). You might want to get to know them as people. Perhaps they are a creative bunch and you want to pick up ideas on style, an up to date spin on life, or whatever. Maybe you feel isolated in your study and want to discover where the issues are for a group of ordinary Christians setting out to bring this particular truth to life in their careers, homes and families. My guess is – and it is only a guess – that you will be more effective in helping the team to learn if they realise that you want to learn something through the experience, too.

Working with a bunch of young chaps from church taught me a lot about how young people today think. I found out a little bit about why reverence is hard. It isn't simply that Christian young people set out to be irreverent. It is almost as if something is missing from the generational mindset. It can be re-awakened. But the experience helped my understanding.

I'm still at the stage where I have to consciously stop myself from getting too involved in producing material. I have to work hard to think about where the group needs to go and to find ways of helping it to find its own way there. I think it is hard. But when the light goes on, when someone finally sees it for himself or herself, when someone goes out and buys a book on the topic, when you discover a couple has spent hours discussing the material, when someone cannot sleep afterwards because the ideas keep buzzing around, then you know it was worth it.

Time

We have talked a lot about technique, but the most important thing you can give anyone is your time. Not quality time – just time. Time for them to watch and have a go. Time for them to get to know you, to see you get excited, to see you when you are down, to understand what it is about the task that upsets, worries, frustrates or angers you. Time to talk things over – to make friends.

It was time, more than anything else, that Jesus gave his disciples. But, you say, time is the one thing I don't have! Time is why I need fifteen assistants and a PA. Time is why my kids have given up asking me to fix their lego toys. Time is why my wife is mad at me right now. That's why I said it doesn't have to be quality time. You can use the time in the car. I actually think mobile phones are great if they are used properly. By properly, I mean you keep them switched off with a voicemail message that you check a couple of times a day. You switch them on when you want to talk. They are not quite cheap enough to use for private, non-quality time conversations – but they are almost there.

Hands free, of course, while you are stuck in traffic, you will be able to touch base with lots of people, once the price is right. If I am driving for work, I like to get some of the longer conversations going by phone. I am not putting my conversational partner under time pressure. There is time to think through what is happening. I am not sure I would wish to conduct a detailed piece of bargaining around the M25, but there is a lot I can do. Cordless phones work all over the house – while you are doing the dishes (provided the family is elsewhere) even in the bath.

How about shopping together? Washing the cars together? Just doing things that you have to do anyway, but doing with someone. Driving to and from events that you have to go to anyway. Filling the car up with people might militate against spending the time you want to with an individual. Perhaps this is your excuse to buy a sports car or one of those cute town cars that everyone seems to have brought to market in the last fortnight.

If you can use your time that way, you will feel less driven when you cannot go out tonight because you want to spend time at home, or when you leave the phone ringing because you are reading to the kids.

So how do I start?

Well where are you? If you are not doing much by way of serving God, the first step may be to find a mentor. Who looks busy? Who is overloaded? Whom does everyone go to when they need something done?

Perhaps you are involved in something already. Is it fun? Can you share that fun with someone else? Could you start to work yourself out of it now?

The only way I know to get started is to start. To accept that you will make mistakes. To take whatever hints or training are going with gratitude. To pray about it. To think about it. To trust that if you are praying and acting, God will bless and multiply the right adventures and quietly shut down the unhelpful ones.

Part of that trusting might involve talking to your vicar, or a Christian friend. Part of it might involve asking God to create the first opening of an opportunity. It might mean getting your home group to pray it through with you. I don't know how it will work out, but the combination of prayer, trust and thoughtful action is potent stuff.

Of course, you might be the wrong sort of person to get into mentoring. Maybe you are driven by a poor self-image and wish to be seen to be doing something. You may have tried half a dozen things recently and see this as the next new thing, not realising that you are at the mercy of frustrations elsewhere in your life. If it doesn't work, don't despair. If no-one follows it might be because you are not the leader you would like to have been. Maybe there is a different role for you in something that someone else is up to. I can't look into your life and see where you stand. In writing to encourage you, I take the risk that this will lead you personally to take the wrong step. I'm sorry.

I remember a cartoon in which the lead character was reading about all the foods that were bad for you. At first, he concluded that eating could kill you. However, in the end realised it would not kill you as fast as not eating.

On the whole, it's the same here. The dangers of doing nothing outweigh the dangers of having a go – by about a million to one. Enjoy.

Thinking it through

1. How would a Christian approach to mentoring differ from that practised, say, by a Buddhist master?
2. In what ways is being a mentor at church different from mentoring at work? Is it the same in any way?
3. What was St. Paul like as a mentor? Find three incidents or steps that Paul took, which illuminate his mentorship of Timothy?
4. In what respects would Apollos (Acts 18:24-28) have been a hard person to mentor? Why did Priscilla and Aquila believe he needed some help? How did they provide it?
5. List three skills or areas of experience that fewer than five other people have at your church. How could you be involved in helping others to gain them?
6. How did you spend the time on your last three car journeys? How might you have spent it better?
7. What chore or activity do you do at least once a month that you could usefully do with another Christian – either to help them or to benefit from being with them? How could

you start to do things together?

8. If you could have spent a year with Moses, what would you have liked to have learnt from him? Whom could you learn it from today?

7

The School Bell

One Christmas a school friend of mine gave me a poster on which a number of hippopotamuses stood around, mouths wide open in the heat of an African afternoon. The motto explained that, after all was said and done, a lot more was said than done. I never knew quite why he chose it. I was certainly a great talker. There were times when he felt compelled to find quieter spots in the library because my chat got in the way of his study. He has gone on to great success in a very brainy discipline. I had never thought of myself as a non-doer, however. Perhaps he just liked the hippos.

And one of the dangers of writing a book is that yet more will be said but on the whole not a great deal more done. When we looked at what Jesus' disciples had in common, we noted that they were all products of the same Jewish school system and that they were all doing something else. We could have noted one other thing. They were all chaps. I do not want to explore the question of whether Jesus would have restricted his choice in the same way had he been calling disciples today.

But I want to take a little time out in this book to talk particularly to men. On average, Christian men seem happier to leave Christian service to Christian women, than to engage in it themselves. This last feature has been true for most of the (last) century. Even today, you have only to look at the picture galleries missions publish of their new recruits or short-term workers to notice the dearth of happy chappies – or indeed chappies of any sort. A friend of mine runs WEC Trek, an effort aimed at giving people a short but complete package of training and practical experience of mission life. She is worried right now that there will be no men at all for the next event. The same sort of picture applies at home where women get on with so many of the tasks in local churches.

Ah! Perhaps it is because women live longer. After all, with an extra 5% or so of life, maybe there should be 5% more of them about. With skill and low cunning, we might even manage to explain away a 10% discrepancy. Our only problem is that we need to explain a discrepancy in the ranks of Christian service of perhaps 50% or more.

Our willingness, as men, to commission women to go to the toughest parts of the world and serve unstintingly for a lifetime is a characteristic we share with our fathers and, indeed, grandfathers.

It has been going on for long enough to have disturbed most thinking Christians into finding some sort of answer. I don't know what the real answers are but I think it is worth reminding this generation of men, that Jesus called men and, first time around, they left their work behind and followed.

Why don't we follow, too?

So why do we, as men, find the call to do something so hard? Perhaps it is something to do with that tricky tension which Jesus touched on, 'You cannot serve God and Money' (Luke 16:13).

You have probably wondered how Jesus thought anyone could mix up something as mundane as money with the immortal, invisible, God. At every point, the contrast between the two is as dramatic as it is obvious. Physical against spiritual. The decaying (and latterly eroding through inflation) against the eternal. The answer lies in the way each affects us. Each awakes an instinct within us to serve: one in worry, the other in worship. And I think that tension is particularly exquisite for men today, although it has been effective down through the ages. It would be crass to suggest that Christian materialism is down to one sex, but the modern twists seem to be particularly deadly for blokes.

After all, we have to make our way in the real world. It takes commitment to survive the cutbacks and hang onto your rung of the ladder as wave after wave of rationalisation washes over you. It often takes long hours. Then there is that status thing, too. What sort of lifestyle do the other blokes expect of you? What do you deserve yourself? The result is a strong focus on ourselves and on our careers. The tricky tension Jesus knew all about grows taut.

Billy Joel sang, 'I have been a fool for lesser things.' And, as all songwriters do, he manages to speak for a generation hooked on lesser things. If our job is the serious side of life, we long to be distracted by constellations of gizmos and gadgets. I know: I love them too. We love the latest laptops, with whizzo graphics for animated presentations. We love acceleration, trip computers, in-car entertainment systems and those extra few square centimetres of wheel base. We love our sport. It is amazing how broad-minded we can be when it comes to sport, accommodating the disparities of football, cricket, tennis, a spot of swimming, maybe, formula one, cycling, athletics, and to slow our racing pulses, a few frames of snooker, or even bowls, to draw our day to a close. I could watch sport all day. Perhaps, as Jerome K Jerome observed, it is the sight of someone else working so hard. My wife doesn't have this problem (although she has become alarmingly knowledgeable on the football front in the past few years).

Add to this the loss of confidence about what it means to be a man. I caught a snatch of an article in yesterday's paper. The journalist was urging Sophie Rhys Jones not to promise to obey Prince Edward in the vows they plan to exchange imminently. He argued that most thirty-something blokes do not want to make the tough decisions on their own. The alarming thing is the reticence with which they face up to any decisions at all. Marriage goes on hold because he isn't sure he is ready for it. Marriage goes pop as he suddenly discovers he is a party animal after all, and needs all the time he can get for his mates after work and a recharge at the weekend.

And still to men in our generation, careerwise committed, easily distracted and confused about their role in life, comes the call to leave lesser things and serve the King of Kings.

What if...?

What would be the effect of thousands of men deciding that Jesus is worth engaging with seriously? That, if you have to put in the hours, you might as well invest them in eternity rather than the next car, house, or diversion? What would happen if a tide of chaps swept through our churches, willing to take on something – anything, willing to lay their gifts and training at the disposal of that Someone who started out with a few fishermen two millennia ago?

I guess my prejudices on how churches should work would

come out sooner or later. I believe in churches where everyone gets stuck in. Not just the women. Not just at weekends. I'm not saying that you have to fill your weeknights with meetings but it is all too easy to turn our week into a no-go area, firstly for church, and ultimately for our faith.

Back to the plot...

Imagine churches with a surfeit of leaders – a generation in service, a generation getting ready, and the next generation already in view – a bit like the planes coming in at Heathrow on a busy evening. Do you think we might be able to double and split? Do you think we might see growth in numbers? Might we see growth in character? A bit more fruit, maybe?

Of course, denominationalism doesn't really come into it. Alpha encompasses some of these principles, and Alpha is Anglican at heart. A structured form of leadership has given birth to a very group-oriented way forward. While independent churches have been getting their leadership act together by adding pastors or full-time workers to their leadership teams, many more formal denominational groups are exploring team ministries, elevating lay ministries and generally spreading the burden. Great!

Of course it won't take off until people, ordinary people, face up to Jesus, find out what he wants of them and quietly get on with it. The Roman Empire gave way before the early church, not because Christians had a better PR machine, better policies, or superior communications. It caved in ultimately because Christianity worked. The Holy Spirit changed people and they lived out that change. Ultimately, the effect of thousands, tens of thousands, millions of lives lived for Jesus proved to be unstoppable.

We have some wonderful opportunities for 'big' Christianity today – through the media, in high profile events, with publicly recognised names. And these provide wonderful opportunities to bring Jesus to masses of people. I remember heading off early one morning and catching a piece of the farming programme on Radio 4. Some vicar was into rogation services and they sang 'Jesus is Lord, Creation's voice proclaims it!' I thought it was great. I thought of thousands of sleepy commuters making their way towards or along the M25, growing sentient that morning to the sound of this bold vicar and his congregation singing their hearts out around some farmyard. Top!

But I guess my burden is for 'small' Christianity. The sort of faith that seizes the challenge and gets on with it, day in, day out. The sort that grows at the edges as more people are pulled in. The sort that costs so much more to so many more people, because small Christianity is expensive Christianity. It costs time. My time, your time. It means standing up to be counted. It means wrestling with priorities.

This book cannot help to get to grips with that challenge. Ultimately, you throw yourself in because Jesus has called and you want to respond. People do things with Jesus because they want to, and for no other reason.

What I hope this book might help you with, is to see how you might get involved. I hope it will excite you about the possibilities of using the things God has given you by way of gift and training, in Christian service. You may not yet relish the prospect of getting stuck in, but I hope that you have lost the excuse that you have nothing to offer.

School is out. It's time for work.

Thinking it through

1. Where does 'big' Christianity work best? Why?
2. What gifts, skills and training has God given you? What would it cost you to focus them into one avenue of service?
3. Why did you become a Christian? How has your relationship with Jesus changed since? How will you find out where Jesus wants to take the relationship next?
4. Are you going to do anything specific as a result of reading this book? What? By when?

8

In The End

Well, it's all over. Perhaps I can offer a couple of words of explanation before signing off for good.

I may come across as someone who has things sussed. I haven't. I had not realised that trying to write down what you thought you believed could be such a creative or exploratory experience. I guess I thought that you did something, or believed something and then you wrote it down. Here I have often found that the opposite is also true. Sometimes I have found myself discovering what the Bible says about an issue and then later, in a spot of difficulty, trying to put what I have written into practice. And I have been amazed at times, at how helpful the whole process is. I have a friend who, while at art school, told me that he used to draw with his eyes shut – to surprise himself. There have been times here when I have been surprised myself. In a sense, I'm starting out to try and make more sense of all this stuff, too. I'm excited about more experiments.

My second concern is that you might think that the church at which I worship is in some way special. If this book has challenged you, you might conclude that my church will be a very well-led church. The leadership will be well focused and exercising a range of gifts and skills to the great benefit of the fellowship as a whole. The church will be responding to the challenge to exercise its gifts and training and the whole place will be buzzing (should you ever discover where we live) on arrival.

The problem with my church, of course, is that I go to it. And I have an infinite capacity for messing up. My church isn't any better than yours – and for much the same reasons. Ironically, the areas in which the church where I worship does well are largely those areas where I have least influence. If you find us and visit us, you may well be moved, though I suspect it will involve disappointment and surprise in roughly equal measure.

But, and there is a but, my church, like your church is part of the great church that Jesus is building. He likes it. He loves it. One day it will be perfect.

Further Reading

1. Roy Clements, *The Strength of Weakness*, Christian Focus Publications, 1994
2. James Dunn, *The Effective Leader*, Kingsway Publications, 1995
3. Mark Greene, *Thank God it's Monday*, Scripture Union, 2nd edition, 1997
4. Rob Parsons, *The Sixty Minute Father*, Hodder & Stoughton, 1995
5. Neil Summerton, *A Noble Task*, The Paternoster Press 2nd edition, 1994